SevenSecrets
of

P
E
R
F
E
C
T

Parenting

Shelly Herold, M.S., Ed.

Published by Frederick Fell Publishers, Inc.
www.fellpub.com

While insights and suggestions in this book are based on professional experience and research with children and parents, they are not intended to replace the advice of your physician or health care provider who knows you and your child's individual medical history. The author and publisher will not bear any responsibility for liability, loss or risk, personal or otherwise that is incurred as a direct or indirect consequence of any information in this book.

Stories in this book are not based on specific individuals, but include composites of many persons and situations; names and pronouns (he/she) have been arbitrarily assigned.

Library of Congress Cataloging-in-Publication Data

Herold, Shelly.
  Seven secrets of P.E.R.F.E.C.T parenting / Shelly Herold.
     p. cm.
  Includes bibliographical references and index.
  ISBN 0-88391-101-9 (trade pbk. : alk. paper)
  1. Child rearing. 2. Parenting. I. Title: Seven secrets of PERFECT parenting. II. Title.
  HQ769.H5157 2004
  649'.1--dc22

                            2004005468

Front Cover Photo by: Claus Wickrath
Cover/Interior Design by Chris Hetzer
Printed in USA

10 9 8 7 6 5 4 3 2 1

ENCOURAGE, ENRICH, AND EXPERIENCE LIFE
WITH YOUR CHILD FROM INFANCY AND BEYOND

SevenSecrets
of
P
E
R
F
E
C
T
Parenting

Shelly Herold, M.S., Ed.

Dedication

With heartfelt love and affection, I dedicate this book to:

- my extraordinary children, David Marc and Caryn Michele, who have taught me that "input really does = output"

- my beautiful grandchildren, Morgan Layne and Adam Gabriel, who have shown me the miracle of life all over again

- my husband, Fred, who has confirmed my belief that "getting in-sync" with love, empathy, and consistency are basic to perfect parenting.

"Shelly Herold has drawn upon her vast fund of knowledge and experience to create a wonderfully insightful and unique guide to parenting. This book is a true standout that will prove to be an invaluable aid to all those parents fortunate enough to include it in their library."

Gary Birken, M.D., Pediatric Surgeon; Associate Director of Medical Affairs, Joe DiMaggio Children's Hospital; Fellow, American Academy of Pediatrics; Fellow, American Pediatric Surgical Association; Author

"This is a must-read book for all parents - the simplicity of the approaches are likely to be met with a lifetime of family harmony and child-rearing success."

Richard Derman, M.D., M.P.H.; Schutte Chair, Associate Dean of Women's Health, Professor of Obstetrics and Gynecology, University of Missouri - Kansas City School of Medicine

"As a working mother, this book has become an incredible resource, filled with tips and solutions for balancing the needs of my family with my career."

Allison L. Friedman, Esq., Attorney and Past President of Coral Gables Bar Association

"Someone has finally revealed the secrets to perfect parenting in a responsible, exciting, and informative manner. Shelly Herold, a consummate early childhood educator, has given parents a realistic roadmap to follow in raising their children to become sociable, successful. Her work deserves the highest praise."

Rabbi Robert P. Frazin, D.D., Spiritual Leader of Temple Solel, Hollywood, Florida; former Advisor to the Ohio Valley Federation of Temple Youth and the Southeast Federation of Temple Youth

"What a great gift for every new or expectant parent! Shelly Herold's book is packed with creative strategies to help mothers and fathers provide their children with love, care, and intellectual stimulation."

Debbie Bass, B.A., B.S. Ed., Director, Montessori Children's World, Las Vegas, Nevada

"Shelly Herold's book provides a wealth of practical advice and tips to those parents motivated in being the best parents they can be."

Marshall Ohring, M.D., American Academy of Pediatrics, Fellow; Board Certified in Pediatrics; Private Practice

"Mrs. Herold has succeeded in exploring all the important issues of good parenting in an easy-to-read, memorable fashion. This book will be an invaluable tool for even the busiest of parents in their quest to raise healthy, happy children."

Crystal A. Dillard, M.S.W., F.S.O.S.W., Counselor, Jupiter Hospital, North Palm Beach, Florida

"Every parent (or grandparent) can benefit from the practical advice in this book. It would have been helpful when my kids were young, but now I can use it profitably with my grandchild."

Norman Grover, M.D., Ophthalmologist, Fellow, American College of Surgeons

Contents

Acknowledgments

While enjoying a fulfilling career as Director of Early Childhood Education and Programming in a South Florida Private School, I have had the pleasure of sharing twenty-five years of intellectual, creative, and social experiences with thousands of young children and their parents. As they chatted in my office to convey personal anecdotes and attended my parenting lectures to seek guidance, these mothers and fathers also prompted me to write, "Seven Secrets of P-E-R-F-E-C-T Parenting," and I am grateful.

Their children who attended my pre-kindergarten, kindergarten, and performing arts classes particularly inspired me. While each one was unique, all were amazingly curious and shared the common desire to be nurtured, hugged, enriched, and encouraged. As I reached within myself to motivate every one of them, I watched them thrive and came to understand the best techniques for developing the "total" child: these approaches are featured throughout this book for every parent to explore.

Balancing career, marriage, and parenting has taught me to prioritize, organize, and to be thankful for help from my family and friends. Thank you Joe Snyder, Sara Aronow, Michael Chasin, Joan and Dr. Bob Cohen for your motivation. Thanks, Don Lessne, Fell Publishing, for your immediate acceptance and Chris Hetzer, graphic design.

Special thanks, Fred, for sharing thirty-seven years of devotion and support for my philosophy that, "love, care, and attention create the "perfect" environment in which to develop happy, healthy, and successful children." Thanks, David and Caryn for always making us proud; your educational and career accomplishments are only superseded by your exuberant personalities and compassion as human beings, as marriage partners for Melissa and Wade, and now, as parents of Adam and Morgan. Thank you for proving my "seven secrets" really work!

Shelly Herold

Shelly Herold |

Getting Ready for the Best Job Ever

1. Anticipating Your New Career as a Parent

Let's face it; being a parent is a monumental task. As you welcome your "beautiful, little miracle" into the world, your life changes drastically and you will never, ever be the same. The arrival of your baby announces your most important job promotion. Congratulations! You are about to begin the work of a lifetime.

Photo By:Claus Wickrath

THE MOST PRECIOUS BABY IN THE WHOLE WORLD IS WAITING FOR YOUR WARMTH, LOVE, AND NOURISHMENT.

Your new career as a parent will require:

▼ **Organizational skills of an executive**
▼ **Enthusiasm of a cheerleader**
▼ **Patience of a teacher**
▼ **Sensitivity of an artist**
▼ **Dedication of a physician**
▼ **Strategy of a world leader**

Perhaps you are wondering, "Do I have what it takes? Can I do it all? How can I feel more self-assured? Did someone say parenting was easy? HELP!!!"

Your feelings are not unusual. Most new Moms and Dads share your anxiety, but relax. You're already on track. You are curious about your new responsibility and you are seeking information to help you become more knowledgeable and competent.

2. Discovering the Seven Secrets

"Seven Secrets of **P-E-R-F-E-C-T** Parenting" will help you find your hidden strengths, improve your feelings of self-confidence, and provide you with the wisdom necessary to become more efficient and proficient in balancing all of life's challenges. As you and your spouse gain emotional grounding and the necessary organizational skills, you will both feel less stressed, happier, and ready to nurture and love your baby in the best possible environment.

Within each of the seven approaches to great parenting, you will discover tips to help you engage your child in both warm and exciting experiences from infancy onward. You will gain insights towards understanding your baby's sounds and gestures and hints to assist you in reaching out with caring compassion. Then you and your baby will feel a sensitive connection beyond bonding; you will be "in-sync" with each other's needs and feelings. Your special relationship will lead to mutual thoughtfulness and respect. Only then will you be able to enhance your youngster's total, unique potential.

HELPFUL HINTS:

❖ Get in touch with your child's individuality to best direct his/her development

❖ Respond to your son or daughter consistently with love to enjoy a lifetime of healthy interactions.

Can you be *perfect*? Can you raise the *perfect* child? Realistically, no one can be flawless and totally ideal, but a genuine interest in the topic of parenting and the realization that it takes a great deal of work is the best beginning.

Let the word, **"P-E-R-F-E-C-T"** be your guide.

"P" = PRIORITIZE 1

Despite all the stories you have heard about the difficulties of raising a child in the past, you will surely experience a more complicated parenting challenge today. Historically, the family unit was simple and parental roles were clear: Dad worked, Mom handled the kitchen and the kids, and grandparents often lived nearby to lend a hand.

In the late 1960's, the Women's Liberation Movement paved the way for female achievement in the workplace and family life was forever changed. Women clamored up corporate ladders, initiated creative ventures, applied their talents outside the home and moved toward job opportunities, often far from family. As they rejoiced in their new career freedom and equality with men, females faced an unforeseen consequence, the stress of juggling a job, the house, marriage and the children. Their spouses, unaccustomed to household chores or participation in childrearing also met with new, unexpected responsibilities, and grandparents were no longer close by to help.

Today, most individuals multi-task, but while they strive for self-fulfillment and success in every endeavor, they still wonder, "Is it possible to balance it all?"

Of course it is. Simply join with your partner and start with the letter, **"P,"** in the word **P-E-R-F-E-C-T.**

Secret # 1

"PRIORITIZE"
ORGANIZE YOUR LIVES BY FOCUSING ON THE MOST IMPORTANT THINGS FIRST

Priorities change when you initiate a new stage in your life. While a student, you are concerned with your studies, and as an employee, you aspire towards job accomplishment. In the early months of a loving relationship, you concentrate on your soul mate. When you become expectant parents, you change your focus once again and prepare for your future addition.

1.The Well-Being of Your Child is Your First Priority

Since your infant will be totally helpless and dependent upon you for bodily comfort, good health, emotional security, and happiness, it is advantageous for you to get your lives and your home in order before your son or daughter's arrival. Remember, **WHEN YOU BECOME A PARENT, YOU ARE RESPONSIBLE FOR MAINTAINING THE WELL-BEING OF YOUR CHILD WITH BASIC PHYSICAL CARE, SENSITIVITY, AND LOVE. IT IS UP TO YOU TO MEET YOUR BABY'S NEEDS UNSELFISHLY; THIS IS YOUR FIRST PRIORITY.** How do you begin to meet this overwhelming challenge?

✱ Preparing for Your Newborn

When you realize that your baby is coming, you will instinctively modify your way of life, your home, your interests, feelings, and relationships.

Changing Your Lifestyle and Your Home

Whether you previously enjoyed late parties, athletic vacations, unusual food, shopping for the latest fashions, intensive workouts in the gym, working late in the office, or simply following a nine to five work schedule and relaxing at home each evening, you will now modify your lifestyle and prepare for your arrival.

Until now, your living quarters seemed perfectly adequate and attractive, but with the expectation of an additional family member, you may decide to shuffle furniture, empty closets, paint lamps, shelves and walls.

LIKE NEST-BUILDING BIRDS INSTINCTIVELY PRIMED TO WELCOME THEIR OFFSPRING, YOU AND YOUR SPOUSE WILL ARRANGE A WONDERFUL ROOM OR CREATE A COZY CORNER FOR YOUR LITTLE ONE.

How will you arrange your infant's belongings, the playpen and the toys? Do you need a screen to section an existing room? Should you consider building a wall or moving to a larger place? Perhaps, you are in need of an extra bed, linens, and closet space because you are hiring a baby nurse or a nanny, or an excited Grandma is coming to help for three weeks. There are so many things to do and buy.

New Interests, New Priorities

It's amazing! Everyone seems to be pregnant or pushing a stroller. Neighbors you never even noticed before have sparked your attention because they have babies or toddlers. Suddenly you are aware of children in restaurants and you begin to wonder about your unborn infant. Will her hair be dark and curly or blond and straight? Will he have blue or brown eyes? Will he embarrass you and scream in public places like that kid throwing a tantrum at the next table?

You remark about the cute pattern on the diaper bag of that incredibly thin mother. How did she get her figure back so soon? Your spouse notices the father running in circles to retrieve the toys that his son tosses on the floor from the high chair. Your perception, interests, and priorities are changing.

You visit maternity shops to find the most fashionable outfits, take your partner through stores that specialize in infant layettes, baby gear, and scrutinize the checklists they happily provide for your convenience. You sit for an hour to complete the baby registry for family and friends and each time your baby kicks, you grab your spouse's hand to feel the motion. It is not unusual to be submerged in decision making as you view the vast variety of cribs, complementary furniture and accessories, colorful paints, wallpaper and borders, linens, curtains, baby outfits, mobiles, toys, strollers, etc.

HELPFUL HINTS:

VIEW SHOPPING AS A SPECIAL ADVENTURE TO SELECT THE VERY FIRST THINGS YOU WILL SHARE WITH YOUR CHILD AND PLAN A COMFORTING ENVIRONMENT THAT APPEALS TO THE SENSES:

❖   Soft things to **SURROUND & TOUCH**

❖   Colorful, moving toys to **SEE & STIMULATE**

❖   Soothing music to **HEAR & REASSURE**

❖   Feeding supplies to provide **NOURISHMENT & TASTE**

SELECT A FEW NECESSITIES BEFORE BABY'S ARRIVAL

- Bathtub, Bibs, Blankets, Boppy Pillow, Bottles, Bouncy Chair, Brushes, Bumpers, Burp Cloths.
- Cameras (for stills and video), Car seat, Changing pad and table/dresser, Chest, Cotton pads/swabs, Creams, Crib.
- Detergent (gentle for babies), Diapers, Diaper Bag, Diaper Pail.
- Educational books and playthings (developmentally appropriate).
- Formula (unless you plan to totally breastfeed)
- Glider (or Rocker) and ottoman, Gowns.
- Hats, High chair, Hooded Towels.
- Lamp, Layette (soft, comfortable clothing), Linens (pads, sheets, curtains)
- Mattress, Monitor, Musical Mobile, CDs/DVDs (lullabies and children's songs).
- Nail Clippers, Night Light, Nipples.
- Pacifiers, Play seat/rocker, Playpen, Pump.
- Shampoo/Soap (for babies), Sheets, Sterilizer, Stroller, Sweaters.
- Thermometer, Toys (for bath, car seat, crib, floor, stroller).
- Washcloths, Wipes.

New expenses can be brutal, even for couples who are financially secure: Mom's new clothing, Baby's layette, physician and hospital fees, pharmaceutical and pediatric bills, the cost of additional help in the home, coupled with the temporary or permanent loss of dual income.

SEARCH FOR THE BEST BUYS, BUT ALWAYS CONSIDER "SAFETY"

Whether choosing new furniture or receiving used pieces from family or friends:

- Obtain smooth finishes (no splinters), non-toxic paint, rounded corners, sturdy shelves and legs, tightened screws and drawer pulls, safety-approved cribs and frames (slat spaces not to exceed 2 3/8 inches apart).
- Acquire a clean and firm crib mattress.
- Review instructions before assembling all furniture; lock all parts securely.
- Speak to other parents about their experiences with stores and products.
- Read current consumer research literature carefully before purchasing.
- Remain attentive to media broadcasts of malfunctions and recalls.

Sharing Feelings and Relationships

With female hormones raging in a changing body, expenses rising, responsibilities increasing, both wife and husband cannot help but experience a wide range of mixed emotions prior to the birth of the baby. "Am I ready for a child? Will I make a good parent? Will my baby be healthy? Will I know what to do?" You are not the first individuals to have these doubts so do not hesitate to share your feelings with others.

TALK ABOUT YOUR UNCERTAINTIES, CLARIFY CONCERNS, AND LESSEN YOUR FEARS:

✦ **SHARE YOUR THOUGHTS AND EMOTIONS WITH YOUR PARTNER AND MAINTAIN AN EXCITED, OPTIMISTIC OUTLOOK TOGETHER;** you will both feel better and ready for your new addition.

✦ **SCHEDULE THE NEXT SONOGRAM AND OBSTETRICIAN'S APPOINTMENTS WHEN BOTH SPOUSES CAN ATTEND;** enjoy the amazement of seeing your unborn child and prepare a list of questions for the physician or the assistant.

✦ **ATTEND BIRTHING CLASSES TOGETHER AND DEMYSTIFY THE DELIVERY PROCESS;** you will feel less frightened when know what is about to happen.

✦ **SOCIALIZE WITH OTHER SOON-TO-BE PARENTS OR VISIT COUPLES WHO HAVE RECENTLY HAD A BABY;** you will have lots to talk about, lots to learn.

✦ **REACH OUT TO YOUR OWN PARENTS OR IN-LAWS;** having a baby often brings you closer to your family. Perhaps, Mom or Dad will reveal humorous stories of your arrival or help relieve your anxiety by sharing shopping experiences. This event is meaningful for them too, particularly if your son or daughter will be one of the first grandchildren.

✦ **IF YOU ARE EMPLOYED, DISCUSS YOUR POSITION WITH YOUR SUPERVISOR AS TO TIME AWAY FROM YOUR JOB AND YOUR PLANS TO RETURN.** Will they hire a replacement for you or allow your co-workers to pitch in and help? Can you work from home one or two days each week? Is it possible to come back to your job on a part time basis at first?

Is your spouse able to take some "paternity leave" too? "The Family and Medical Leave Act (FMLA)," entitles both spouses, by law, to enjoy an adjustment time with the new arrival. However, each state and each place of employment will maintain and uphold different guidelines.

HELPFUL HINT:

ORGANIZE YOUR LIVES BEFORE YOUR LITTLE ONE ARRIVES AND GET A HANDLE ON THE MANY CHANGES WITHIN YOURSELVES, YOUR HOME, YOUR ROUTINES, YOUR WORK, AND YOUR RELATIONSHIPS WITH FAMILY, FRIENDS, AND COLLEAGUES.

Place everything into perspective, **PRIORITIZE**, and you will be prepared for your parenting role.

✱ Adjusting Your Lives

WHEN YOUR BRING YOUR BEAUTIFUL BABY HOME FOR THE FIRST TIME, YOU WILL EXPERIENCE THE REALITY OF BEING A MOTHER OR FATHER. As you and your spouse welcome your son or daughter into your lives, you will surely feel exhilaration for the moment and anticipation for all that is yet to be.

Parenting, particularly during the early years, will capture a tremendous amount of your time and energy. Diapering, feeding, cleansing, comforting, and entertaining your infant and toddler will consume your attention each day and often throughout the night.

Although you and your spouse have already made many changes in your lives and in your home while you awaited your new arrival, you will now realize that the process of adapting to another person in your household has just begun.

YOUR NEW ADDITION WILL CALL FOR YOUR COMPLETE ATTENTION, UNDERSTANDING, FLEXIBILITY, AND LOTS AND LOTS OF PATIENCE.

Jessica left her job in her eighth month of pregnancy to prepare for the big day, but soon became obsessed with watching TV soaps. When she brought Alexa home from the hospital, the new mother was annoyed because the baby always cried during her favorite story and she told her friend, "I'll let her cry. She'll eat when I'm ready."

But Alexa's screams turned into hysteria. When Jessica was ready for her daughter, the newborn was too upset and exhausted to nurse.

This mother was immature and out of touch with her little girl's needs and emotions. Her priorities were inappropriate.

HELPFUL HINT:

YOUR INFANT'S NEEDS DETERMINE A "NATURAL SCHEDULE" FOR SLEEPING, EATING, AND WAKEFULNESS. OBSERVE YOUR BABY'S HABITS AND ADJUST YOUR OWN ROUTINES AROUND YOUR CHILD'S INTERNAL CLOCK TO HELP YOUR LIVES RUN SMOOTHLY FROM THE START.

AS NEW, BUSY PARENTS, YOU WILL PREDICTABLY CHANGE YOUR OWN SCHEDULES FOR EATING, SLEEPING, AND DAILY LIVING:

▼ **YOUR SLEEP PATTERNS.** At first your newborn will nurse every 2 ½ - 3 hours round the clock and you will undoubtedly feel tired; as your baby begins to consume more liquids and sleep longer, you too will gain more rest. At that time, it may be helpful to:

- **SET YOUR MORNING ALARMS ONE-HALF HOUR EARLIER THAN USUAL** to allow each of you to shower and dress while the other is available to respond to your baby's cries.

- **NAP WHEN YOUR BABY NAPS DURING THE DAY.** You will need that time to regain your enthusiasm.

- **CHANGE YOUR BEDTIME TO AN EARLIER HOUR** to accommodate those 2 a.m. and 5 a.m. feedings.

▼ **YOUR EATING HABITS.** Perhaps you are both accustomed to coffee at 8 a.m., but your baby needs some attention at that moment. A joint breakfast may no longer be an option. If you are breastfeeding, you must doubly adapt: eat at a new hour and eliminate coffee from your diet. Your child's schedule will take precedence over your meals.

▼ **YOUR EVERYDAY ACTIVITIES.** Reading the newspaper, watching TV, working out, etc., may not be possible at your usual times. If, however, you have hired a baby nurse, nanny, or are fortunate the have help from a grandparent, your changes will be fewer.

If you feel anxious or confused about all the changes and chores in your life, talk to your spouse about your feelings. When you both agree that your child's well being is your first priority, you will begin to share the common goal of understanding and meeting your baby's needs by forming a parenting partnership to handle everyday errands and childcare. Joint participation will help each of you truly enjoy a balanced lifestyle and the best of parenthood.

TO KEEP YOUR ENERGY LEVEL HIGH AND ANXIETY LEVEL LOW, TAKE TURNS:

- **FEEDING YOUR BABY DURING NIGHTS AND WEEKENDS** with formula or breast milk that has been pumped and refrigerated in advance. Mom can get some rest and Dad can feel closer to his child.

- **STIMULATING YOUR BABY'S SENSES** with a rattle, a musical mobile, a puppet, a song, while your loved one reads the newspaper, has a massage, or relaxes in the tub.

- **CUDDLING YOUR BABY IN YOUR ARMS OR IN A ROCKING CHAIR** while your husband/wife speaks on the phone to friends or family.

- **SHOPPING FOR FOOD, HOUSEHOLD NECESSITIES, FORMULA, CLOTHING, GOING TO THE BANK, THE PHARMACY.** If you are a stay-at-home parent, you will particularly welcome a change of scenery and time out.

- **PREPARING DINNER OR PICKING UP PREPARED FOOD** while the other parent rests or visits with a friend. One spouse may truly enjoy the role of "Chef."

- **CLEANING BOTTLES, CHANGING DIAPERS, CRIB SHEETS, WASHING BABY'S CLOTHES.** Your partner can get a haircut, manicure, play tennis, or prepare a report for work.

- **PHOTOGRAPHING/VIDEO TAPING YOUR CHILD AND SPOUSE** to capture wonderful memories with each parent.

ALWAYS BATHE YOUR BABY TOGETHER EACH NIGHT

This pre-bedtime routine is a loving, pleasurable activity that will relax your child and ease the task for one adult.

You and your spouse will feel closer to each other and to the baby as you jointly share the duties of childcare and reduce your feelings of anxiety.

As a new mother or father you will soon realize that parenthood requires boundless energy in spite of your sleep deprivation, and in addition to the physical challenge, you must often put your own desires aside. Perhaps you are now wondering, "Is my devotion and dedication worth it? If I change my life for my son or daughter today, will it really make a difference in the future?"

❋ Tuning-in to Yourself and Your Baby; Getting "In-Sync"

Many experts have studied individuals from infancy onward and have concluded that early parent-child relationships significantly effect character development and future social behavior. Therefore, it is essential that you are loving and selfless with your newborn, that you try to tune-in to your infant's sounds and signals, try to recognize needs and feelings, and that you "connect," "bond," get close to your baby.

Researchers have shown *three distinctive patterns of child behavior* that result from early mother-child relationships:

A MOTHER'S RESPONSIVENESS TOWARDS HER INFANT WILL DETERMINE HER BABY'S BEHAVIOR AND PERSONALITY

WHEN A MOTHER IS LOVING, CARING, AND RESPONDS QUICKLY TO HER CHILD'S NEEDS FOR FOOD OR COMFORT:

HER BABY BECOMES SECURE, TRUSTING, UNAFRAID TO EXPLORE THE WORLD AND DEVELOPS INTO A HEALTHY, WELL-ROUNDED, INDEPENDENT CHILD.

This child knows, "Mama will come to me if I need help."

IF A MOTHER IS OCCASIONALLY COMFORTING, BUT MORE OFTEN INSENSITIVE AND UNRESPONSIVE TO HER BABY'S CRIES OR SIGNALS OF NEED:

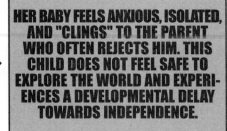

HER BABY FEELS ANXIOUS, ISOLATED, AND "CLINGS" TO THE PARENT WHO OFTEN REJECTS HIM. THIS CHILD DOES NOT FEEL SAFE TO EXPLORE THE WORLD AND EXPERIENCES A DEVELOPMENTAL DELAY TOWARDS INDEPENDENCE.

This infant wonders, "Will my Mama help me if I need her? She usually makes me cry and cry before she comes. I better hold on to her whenever she comes."

WHEN A MOTHER CONSISTENTLY REJECTS HER BABY'S CRIES FOR COMFORT, LOVE, OR BASIC NEED FULLFILLMENT:

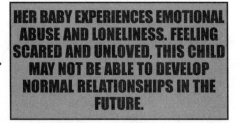

HER BABY EXPERIENCES EMOTIONAL ABUSE AND LONELINESS. FEELING SCARED AND UNLOVED, THIS CHILD MAY NOT BE ABLE TO DEVELOP NORMAL RELATIONSHIPS IN THE FUTURE.

This baby realizes, "No one loves me. No one will help me. I can't depend on anyone." Perhaps this uncaring parent needs psychological help or medication.

Psychologists have also learned that babies require more than nourishment for healthy emotional and physical development; they need to be loved. In one study using infant monkeys, the research team attached feeding bottles with equal amounts of nutrients to "artificial mothers;" one surrogate mother was made of wire and the other of soft, cuddly cloth. The monkeys nursing on the mushy, "cloth mother" were happy, healthy, and playful, but the animals receiving food from the icy, "wire figure" were frightened, anxious, and physically weak. Caring contact is essential from the start.

The literature for the benefits of parental love and responsiveness in the early years is compelling, yet theorists still suggest, "Let your infant cry himself to sleep," or "Do not respond immediately to your sobbing infant." Can this approach possibly be healthy?

Parents during the 1930s were unresponsive to their crying children and stripped them of their spirit. Scared and helpless, these meek babies became non-trusting, powerless men and women with feelings of low self-esteem. Emotions this intense do not go away easily.

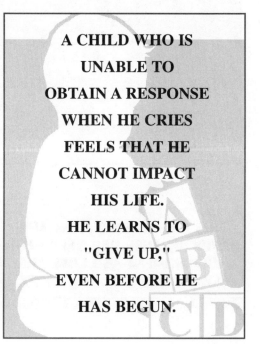

A CHILD WHO IS UNABLE TO OBTAIN A RESPONSE WHEN HE CRIES FEELS THAT HE CANNOT IMPACT HIS LIFE. HE LEARNS TO "GIVE UP," EVEN BEFORE HE HAS BEGUN.

HELPFUL HINT:

DO NOT ABANDON YOUR WEEPING BABY; DRAW UPON YOUR INNER FEELINGS OF COMPASSION, LOVE, AND PATIENCE TO INSURE YOUR CHILD'S WELL-BEING; THIS IS YOUR 1ST PRIORITY.

Your sensitivity will lay the foundation for trust and happiness, for healthy relationships with others in the future.

IT'S AS EASY AS "A, B, C," TO NURTURE YOUR INFANT WITH:

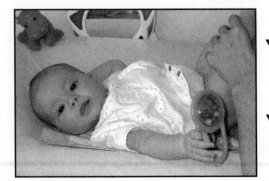

▼**A**FFECTION
Comfort your infant with love, hugs and kisses.

▼**B**ASIC CARE & NUTRITION
Bathe, change, and feed with breast milk or formula, 24 - 7, at the start.

▼**C**OMPASSION
Empathize, understand, respond immediately to cries that signal physical and emotional needs.

THIS INFANT IS CONTENT AND HAPPY BECAUSE HER NEEDS FOR NOURISHMENT AND LOVE ARE ALWAYS MET WITHOUT DELAY.

Isn't it amazing that a human being so tiny can be so complex? Like most new, inexperienced parents, you may find your baby's piercing cries, soft noises, silences, and body language too difficult to interpret. Surely these sounds and motions are expressions of feelings and needs, but what does it all mean? Don't panic! Every new job and every new relationship has a learning curve and requires some time.

USE YOUR SENSES TO BRING YOU CLOSER TO YOUR INFANT:

LOOK into your baby's beautiful eyes; observe that cute, little nose, those delicate lips. Notice the infant's adorable facial expressions and distinctive body movements. Smile and feel delighted! This precious child belongs to you.

LISTEN to the uniqueness of every sound, the cooing, gurgling, crying, burping, and snoring. Why wait for the crying to start? Cuddle your baby when he/she seems content and feel happy because your baby feels good. "Coo and gurgle" right back.

TOUCH your infant gently as you attend to physical needs, wash with a soft cloth and warm water, massage arms, legs, belly, and back with soothing, non-allergenic cream, kiss, hug, and stroke your baby's head and face. Hold your child near to your heart. Feel the warmth and love.

SMELL your baby's uniqueness and deliciousness after a bath. Feel proud of yourself because you are nurturing your baby with affection and care.

As each day passes, you will feel more in-touch with your son or daughter. You will begin to "synchronize your lives" by sharing experiences, by learning to understand each other's voice, movements, smiles and frowns. You will start to build a loving relationship and beyond bonding, you and your child will feel **"IN-SYNC."**

TRY A LITTLE IMAGINATION AND A "MUSICAL MODEL" TO GET "IN-SYNC" WITH YOUR SON OR DAUGHTER:

- Think of your home as a stage for a "MUSICAL SYMPHONY;" you and your spouse are members of the orchestra.

- The "CONDUCTOR" is none other than your little baby giving "CUES," "SOUNDS," "MOVEMENTS," and setting the "MOOD."

- "TUNE-IN" to the leader's "TIMING" and "NATURAL RHYTHM."

- Adjust your own "TEMPO" to be in "HARMONY" with everyone on stage.

- "PRACTICE" every day until you are all "IN-SYNC."

Marge and Peter felt helpless when they first brought baby Sophia home from the hospital and she began to cry. Throughout each day, they listened, "tuned-in" to the baby's various noises, and responded immediately to calm her. Using the "musical model," they paid attention to the pitch, volume, and reverberation of her cries and helped each other understand the meaning of each sound. Sophia was their first priority.

One morning, after three weeks of "practice" as a mother, Marge felt more confident. Sophia's cries at 9:00 a.m. sounded familiar. Almost three hours had passed since the baby's last feeding. Her unpleasant "mood," the sucking "movements" of her lips, and her head turning sideways revealed that she was seeking nourishment. Marge recognized the "cues" and made sense of it all.

*"I know you are hungry. Mommy loves you and feels sad when you cry." She spoke softly to her baby, quickly changed her diaper, and began to breastfeed. **Mother and child were more than connected; they were "in-sync."***

INTERPRETING YOUR BABY'S COMMUNICATIONS

* **YOUR INFANT IS HUNGRY.** Listen to the sound of that cry and look at your baby's tiny hands moving towards his mouth as if to say, "Feed me." His head may be turning sideways, as well, in search of food. Pick up your hungry child and soothe with a song as you pour the formula or prepare yourself for breastfeeding.

* **YOUR INFANT HAS GAS PAINS.** Most often, the intermittent, shrill screams begin some time after a feeding. Look at your infant's face, scrunched and grimacing in discomfort. She pulls her legs up towards her torso or thrashes from side to side. Comfort your little one with gentle pats on the back, with her belly on your shoulder. Walk around the room, tapping and gently rocking until you hear the big burp.

* **YOUR INFANT FEELS UNCOMFORTABLE.** His cries are matched with a unhappy look and fidgety movements. Why is he distressed?

  > **DIAPER RASH?** Perhaps your baby feels a burning sensation in the diaper area. Wash carefully with warm water, dry and treat with an appropriate cream before replacing the diaper.

  > **CHILLED OR OVERHEATED?** If your child feels too hot or too cold you may need to adjust the room temperature and provide a lighter or heavier outfit. (Your lips on the baby's forehead will give you a quick assessment before you get the thermometer.) However, if your child is shivering blue and extremely cold or burning hot, red and flushed, call your doctor immediately while you take your baby's temperature.

  > **CLOTHING TOO SMALL? MATERIAL ROUGH?** Double-check: Is your infant's gown or shirt too tight around the neck, wrists, or ankles? Are garments free of irritating trims or labels? Is the diaper closed too snugly?

❖ **YOUR INFANT IS HAVING A BOWEL MOVEMENT.** You may hear occasional grunting, squeezing noises and notice squirming. When the sounds stop, thoroughly clean your baby's diaper area with several wipes that have been dipped in warm water. Dry the lower body with several soft, cotton pads; apply cream or ointment, and replace the diaper. Your quick attention will avoid a painful diaper rash.

❖ **YOUR INFANT NEEDS A CHANGE OF VIEW, POSITION, OR CRAVES HUMAN CONTACT.** The cries may have a cranky tone. Give your baby a big hug and lots of kisses as you relocate to a blanket on the floor, play a musical CD and sing along, or bring out the toys to amuse. Your smiles and closeness are most important.

❖ **YOUR INFANT IS ILL AND NEEDS A DOCTOR.** If your baby has any of the following: vomiting, diarrhea, persistent crying, unusual breathing, an exceptionally hot and feverish body, or a blue, limp or cold body, do not delay. Call your physician for immediate medical attention.

As you pay attention to those subtle differences in your infant's behavior, you will take an essential step towards getting "IN-SYNC" with your child. Go quickly and happily to the crib before thunderous screams begin, lift your baby up with a big embrace, support that floppy head, softly stroke and kiss that little face. You are bringing comfort, teaching love and dependability. You are also helping your child to feel important, *"MY VOICE HAS BEEN HEARD!"*

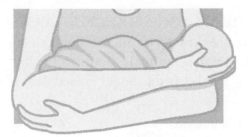

HELPFUL HINT:

YOU CANNOT SPOIL YOUR CHILD WITH TOO MUCH LOVE AND ATTENTION.

Keep your spirits high to provide a pleasant, harmonious environment in which your baby will thrive. If you feel exhausted and unable to bring out the cheerleader inside you, perhaps you are in need of assistance.

When neighbors, Abby and Lila, learned that they were both pregnant, they giggled with joy. Lila, first to deliver, lovingly caressed her infant, affectionately gazed at him and "cooed" even during those two and six a.m. feedings. Although she was tired, the caring Mom synchronized her nap schedule with the baby's and felt thrilled with her little wonder.

Abby's homecoming, on the contrary, was filled with depression and sleeplessness. Sensing his Mom's apprehension, the baby refused to latch on to her breast and cried all day. Her husband tried to console her, but Abby rejected him too.

Lila visited and urged her friend to call the doctor. "Abby, you are not yourself and your family is suffering." She was right. The physician found a hormonal cause and prescribed medication to alleviate her post delivery blues.

HELPFUL HINT:

LIFE WITH YOUR INFANT WILL BE FATIGUING, BUT EXCITING AND WONDERFUL. IF YOUR GLOOM OUT-WEIGHS YOUR HAPPINESS AND YOU FEEL COLD TOWARDS YOUR BABY, YOU MAY REQUIRE SLEEP, MEDICATION, THERAPY, OR SIMPLY NEED SOME HELP AT HOME. SPEAK TO A FAMILY MEMBER, A FRIEND, OR YOUR HEALTH CARE PROVIDER. DO NOT BE EMBARASSED TO ASK FOR ASSISTANCE.

Every new, inexperienced mother needs some support and you do too. Ask your Mother or Mother-in-law to come by in the afternoon to spend some time with the baby so you can rest and refresh for the evening ahead. Perhaps your spouse can leave work two hours earlier than usual twice a week to help you during the first month, or a trusting neighbor can lend a hand. A baby nurse, an Au pair, or a Nanny is a good option, but the cost is usually high. Try to plan ahead and engage someone with a good recommendation to assist you for even a week or two; it may be worth the investment.

ALTHOUGH YOU MAY FIND IT DIFFICULT TO UNDERSTAND YOUR BABY'S FEELINGS, YOUR TINY INFANT WILL SENSE YOUR EMOTIONS AND REACT. She may feel your warmth, snuggle closer and return love. When you and your spouse are calm and happy, your baby will reflect your cheerfulness, but if you are anxious, your infant will echo your discomfort in crankiness. It is therefore, in everyone's best interest to diminish stress, maintain upbeat feelings, and strive for a happy environment.

HELPFUL HINT:

IN THE BEST FAMILY SCENARIO:

❖ **EACH PARENT TUNES-IN TO THE CHILD'S PHYSICAL AND EMOTIONAL NEEDS AND ADJUSTS HIS/HER OWN LIFE TO MEET THESE REQUIREMENTS**

❖ **EACH INDIVIDUAL UNDERSTANDS AND FINDS TIME TO SATISFY HIS/HER OWN EMOTIONS AND WISHES**

❖ **EACH ADULT ALSO REMAINS SENSITIVE TO HIS/HER SPOUSE'S FEELINGS AND NEEDS FOR REST, RELAXATION, AND LOVE**

AS A RESULT, FAMILY MEMBERS ARE PERSONALLY AND MUTUALLY CONTENT.

Can you and your partner find the time to care for yourselves, each other, your marriage relationship, and your baby? Yes you can. PRIORI-TIZE and balance your wishes, needs, and responsibilities. Place yourselves second, immediately after your child on your priority list.

2. Achieving Happiness for You and Your Spouse is Your Second Priority

What makes you feel good? What gives your mate pleasure? How can you both reduce daily pressure? Get more sleep? Perhaps exercise, shopping, a day of beauty, or an evening of romance would provide much needed feelings of satisfaction. For many couples, romance dies with the baby's arrival, but you can keep it alive.

HELPFUL HINT:

TAKE SOME QUIET TIME THIS WEEKEND WHEN YOUR BABY IS ASLEEP, DISCONNECT THE PHONES, GET COZY, AND REALLY TALK TO EACH OTHER ABOUT YOUR TRUE FEELINGS, YOUR NEEDS, AND THOSE THINGS YOU CRAVE TO MAKE YOU HAPPY. DISCUSS IDEAS TO REDUCE YOUR WORKLOAD, MINIMIZE STRESS, AND PROVIDE FUN.

When you both feel relaxed enough to share your personal desires, you may be surprised to learn that your priorities are not the same. Don't be upset. If you can each reduce some tension, you will be ready to revive the happiness that brought you together.

❖ **Indulging Yourselves with Priority Pie**

Simply draw a circle, with seven slices for each day of the week, "priority pie" for the week ahead. List the things that you both must do each day for your child, such as purchase formula, adult food, attend classes with the baby, visit the pediatrician, and those things that you must do for yourselves, see your dentist, conduct a business meeting, visit the in-laws, purchase a gift for a relative, interview housekeepers, etc. Then think about your discussion, your "wish list," and when time permits complete each slice with those 'ingredients' you both need to sweeten your lives: joint massages, soaking in a tub, a hair appointment, a bike ride in the park, a night of bowling, exercising at the gym, renting a movie, a spa treatment, meeting friends at the theater, cuddling, or any luxurious indulgence you can conjure up. Priorities may change weekly, but flexibility is healthy.

PREPARING "PRIORITY PIE," TOGETHER ASSURES THAT YOU:

❖ SHARE AN HONEST DIALOGUE AS YOU TALK, LISTEN, AND COOPERATE WITH ONE ANOTHER REGARDING YOUR NEEDS AND WISHES

❖ BRING ORDER AND ORGANIZATION INTO YOUR LIVES IN A PLAN THAT HELPS YOU BALANCE FEELINGS, ACTIVITIES, AND PRIORITIES

❖ CREATE THE NURTURING, STRESS-FREE ENVIRONMENT NECESSARY FOR RAISING HAPPY CHILDREN

Sample Diagram: Priority Pie for Katie (K) & Mike (M): Week of March 6th

Sunday
K's Family Brunch: 11am Pancake House
K/M: Shop for Rug & week's food;
All: Smith Bar BQ 5 pm

Monday
K/Baby: Gymboree: 9 am
K: Lunch/Mom 12 noon
Work Mtg. 2 pm
Nails: 5:15pm
M: Gym 5:30pm
Order in: Pizza

Tuesday
K: Work Out 5pm
Pick up Dry Cleaning
K/M Boss/Wife 8pm
Dinner at Fish Village
(Pam babysits)

Wednesday
M: Gym/ Pick up wine
K/M: Romantic Eve at Home: 8 pm
K: Cook Steak

Thursday
K/M: Pediatrician 9am
M: Haircut 5:30 pm
TV/relax/ Order in: Chinese Food

Friday
K: Mommy/Me class 9am
K: Work/Lunch Mtg Uptown Office: 12:30
M: Pick up chicken
M/K: Bedtime Massages

Saturday
K: Hair cut 10 am
M: Baby sitting
M's Family Lunch: 12 Noon - Grill Hut
K/M Movie 8 pm
(Pam baby-sits)

After the birth of their infant, Jon was clueless about his wife's feelings. He was certain that she hated her former job and loved staying at home, but Jenny, felt ugly and depressed. "What's happened to me? My hair's drab and thinning, my stomach's bloated, my maternity slacks still fit and I'm exhausted!" When her infant cried that afternoon, she resented Jon who was at work. The baby sensed her anxiety and became fussy at feeding time, but the final blow came that evening. Jon went on and on about an incident in his office and didn't even notice that his wife had prepared his favorite dinner. Jenny exploded, "I need a break!"

The new Mother's feelings were normal. She loved her baby, but needed some help and an empathetic boost of her morale from her husband. They finally talked and prioritized their needs and wishes. Using the pie format, they planned a beauty-shopping time for Mom and a baby-bonding time for Dad each Saturday morning. After the first week, Jenny had a fresh, new hairstyle, a makeover, and two fashionable outfits. She felt so much better and was able to enjoy her time with the baby and her husband.

HELPFUL HINTS:

❖ THE ROLE-SPECIFIC DAYS OF "MOTHERHOOD AND
APPLE PIE" ARE OVER; 21ST CENTURY COUPLES
ORGANIZE THEIR LIVES WITH THOUGHTFUL COOP-
ERATION, WORK AS A TEAM, PLAN EVENTS TO LOOK
FORWARD TO WEEKLY, AND SHARE, "PARENTHOOD
AND PRIORITY PIE."

❖ AS YOU AND YOUR SPOUSE PRODUCE AN INTROSPECTIVE
PLAN TOGETHER AND FOCUS ON YOUR NEEDS AND
WISHES, YOUR LIVES WILL BECOME INCREASINGLY
PRACTICAL, PLEASANT, AND SATISFYING.

PROMOTE FAMILY TOGETHERNESS

IN ADDITION TO PLANNING PRIORITY PIE, SCHEDULE AT
LEAST TWO "DAILY ACTIVITIES" FOR THE ENTIRE FAMILY.
EVERYONE WILL LOVE THE PREDICTABILITY AND FEEL
SECURE:

• ONE MEAL OR SNACK TOGETHER EACH DAY
  Join to eat as a family as soon as your baby can sit in a high chair.

• SOOTHING ROUTINES WITH YOUR CHILD EACH NIGHT
  Share bathing, reading a story, listening to a lullaby, hugging and
  kissing before saying, "Good night."

As your child grows and becomes involved in social occasions, educational activities, music or sports, you will begin to carpool and attend these
proceedings to offer your support and approval. When there are two or
more children in the family, activities begin to overwhelm and overlap.

Planning ahead with "Priority Pie," will help you meet the needs of every family member, thus, creating a loving environment for confident, successful kids. While Mom attends the dance rehearsal with Jenny on Thursday evening, Dad may go to soccer practice with Pete. The following week, each will attend the opposite event. **But, wait. Do you have an adorable doggy or a fluffy little cat? Where does the pet fit in?**

3. Caring for Your Pets is Your Third Priority

Your child is your first priority, your contentment and that of your spouse is your next concern, and if you have a pet, you are responsible for providing food, exercise, activity, grooming, and love.

Pets have needs and feelings too and may suffer jealousy, a form of "sibling rivalry" when you bring the baby home. Remember to:

* INTRODUCE YOUR PET TO THE NEW MEMBER OF THE FAMILY CAUTIOUSLY, allowing the animal to smell the baby's blanket for a day or two before actually revealing the infant

* HOLD YOUR CHILD TIGHTLY AND STROKE YOUR BELOVED DOG OR CAT AT THE SAME TIME as if to say, "We love the baby, but we still love you."

* HAVE A NEW TOY OR TREAT AVAILABLE FOR YOUR PET WHEN MEETING THE NEW ARRIVAL. Your furry one will feel that the baby is connected with something new and special.

* KEEP PETS OUT OF THE BABY'S ROOM TO LIMIT THE INGESTION OF DOG OR CAT HAIR. Ascertain whether your child has difficulty breathing or shows signs of a rash. This may indicate an allergy to animals. Vacuum daily.

* TAKE WALKS WITH BOTH THE BABY AND YOUR DOG; your pet is part of your family and will soon learn to be the baby's protector and friend.

* NEVER LEAVE YOUR BABY ALONE WITH ANY ANIMAL; even a gentle pet is unpredictable.

Photo By: David Herold, M.D.

A CHILD WHO GROWS UP WITH A PET LEARNS TO LOVE, RESPECT, AND CARE FOR ALL LIVING THINGS.

As your child grows, establish a family division of labor so everyone takes part in contributing to the pet's well being. A toddler can learn to place a treat into a bowl or add a cup of water to a saucer. A child growing up in this environment will learn dependability, loyalty, and compassion. If your baby arrives before your pet, however, wait until your son or daughter is old enough to help choose and care for another living creature.

CHILDREN AND PETS REQUIRE A GREAT DEAL OF WORK, COMMITMENT, AND LOTS OF LOVE.

4. Meeting Employment Obligations is an Essential Priority

Earning a living is surely a high priority, but if your job is extremely demanding, limiting your availability for your family, perhaps you need to restructure your work schedule. Particularly when you have an infant who needs you and you are insecure about leaving him, request a meeting with your employer to discuss your dilemma. Give your boss viable alternatives, such as working from home one day each week or leaving earlier once a week and catching up in the evening after your child goes to sleep. Assure your employer that you will meet all of the necessary job responsibilities.

HELPFUL HINT:

AIM TO PRESERVE A HEALTHY BALANCE BETWEEN WORK AND PRIVATE LIFE; REMEMBER THE SEQUENCE OF YOUR PRIORITIES.

William, a successful surgeon, never made it to the breakfast or dinner table and rarely connected with his two sons. "Raising the boys is my wife's job," he told his colleagues as he planned his vacation time, "and she wants to get away from those brats for a couple of weeks."

When his teen son was caught shoplifting, William was startled. "What happened? Why did he steal? I worked so hard to give him everything he wanted." William had made a serious error. His son wanted his father's time and love; he had received neither. Furthermore, the doctor had neither conveyed his values, nor his work ethic to his kids. Only when the boy acted out, did he get what he needed most - notice from his dad.

HELPFUL HINT:

LOVE AND ATTENTION ARE MORE VALUABLE TO A CHILD THAN THE EXTRA MATERIAL THINGS YOU CAN PROVIDE BY WORKING LONGER HOURS. PRIORITIZE "BEING THERE" FOR YOUR SON OR DAUGHTER, FROM THE START.

5. Interacting with Extended Families is a Priority Too

Regular contact with relatives will teach your child the skills of socialization and an increased sense of belonging. Relationships and obligations to family members vary, however, from couple to couple. Only you and your spouse together can determine the extent of involvement with grandparents, aunts, uncles and cousins. Will the interaction be helpful, fun, or stressful? Consider everyone's feelings. The location of your home in relation to family members will usually determine whether one side of the family sees the baby more than the other side. Always be fair on special holidays and birthdays.

GRANDPARENTS, USUALLY VERY PATIENT AND GENEROUS WITH THEIR PRAISE AND ENCOURAGEMENT, LOVE TO TEACH NEW SKILLS TO THEIR CURIOUS, "EAGER-TO-LEARN," GRANDCHILDREN.

GRANDPA AND HIS INFANT GRANDSON ARE PLAYING COMPUTER GAMES.

GRANDMA IS READING A BOOK OF RHYMES TO HER INFANT GRANDDAUGHTER.

PARTICIPATE IN HAPPY FAMILY GET-TOGETHERS WITH BOTH THE MATERNAL AND PATERNAL SIDES

- Alternate holidays between the grandparents' homes.

- Ask one set of grandparents to invite the other grandparents on an occasion and reverse the invitation the following year.

- Host the special happening in your home and invite both sides.

- Plan the event in a restaurant to allow everyone to enjoy your child, the meal, and share in the special day with less work for all.

If you suspect that a situation will be disagreeable, discuss it in advance with your mate and relatives, bring the problems into the open, and agree to meet for a pleasant meal or an activity.

HELPFUL HINT:

IF YOU HAVE A PROBLEMATICAL RELATIONSHIP WITH YOUR PARENT, IN-LAW, OR ANOTHER FAMILY MEMBER, DO NOT DEPRIVE YOUR CHILD OF FORMING A MEANINGFUL RELATIONSHIP WITH THAT INDIVIDUAL. ENCOURAGE A HEALTHY, POSITIVE INTERACTION BY ACTING PLEASANTLY WHEN YOU ARE ALL TOGETHER. IT IS UP TO YOU TO SET THE STANDARDS FOR MATURE BEHAVIOR.

The letter, **"P,"** reminds you and your spouse to, **"PRIORITIZE,"** to arrange your tasks and responsibilities in order of importance, as you see fit. However, your child's welfare should always be your top concern.

In designing **"PRIORITY PIE"** together, you begin to understand the needs and desires of one another and you use your time wisely to balance parenting, marriage, employment and self-satisfaction.

Highlights

"P" = "PRIORITIZE," ORGANIZE YOUR LIVES BY FOCUSING ON THE MOST IMPORTANT THINGS FIRST.

1. PREPARE FOR YOUR NEWBORN:
   - *ADJUST TO CHANGES IN YOURSELVES.*
   - *ADAPT YOUR HOME TO WELCOME YOUR INFANT.*
   - *REVISE WORK SCHEDULES.*
   - *RE-EVALUATE RELATIONSHIPS WITH FAMILY AND COLLEAGUES.*

2. FROM THE MOMENT OF ARRIVAL, YOUR INFANT'S WELL-BEING BECOMES YOUR FIRST PRIORITY:
   - *NURTURE YOUR INFANT with affection, basic care and compassion.*
   - *BE SENSITIVE, RESPONSIVE, AND GET "IN-SYNC" with your child's cues and communications.*

3. ACHIEVING HAPPINESS FOR YOU AND YOUR SPOUSE IS YOUR SECOND PRIORITY:
   - *Design "PRIORITY PIE," together to attain, "A BALANCE OF WORK, MARRIAGE, PARENTING, AND SELF-FULFILLMENT."*
   - **WORK AS A TEAM TO REDUCE STRESS; create a happier, healthier home environment in which to raise successful, cheerful children.**

4. PLAN FOR ADDITIONAL PRIORITIES: PETS, EMPLOYMENT, AND EXTENDED FAMILIES.

" E " = EXPERIENCE LIFE WITH YOUR CHILD **2**

Once you have **"PRIORITIZED,"** determined what is most important in your life, and organized your personal needs and desires each week with "priority pie, you will find the time to:

Secret # 2

"EXPERIENCE LIFE WITH YOUR CHILD"
AND DEVELOP A WELL-ROUNDED, SUCCESSFUL INDIVIDUAL

SHARING EXPERIENCES WITH YOUR SON OR DAUGHTER, FROM INFANCY ONWARD, IS AN EXCITING, REWARDING, AND POWERFUL ASPECT OF PARENTING. THROUGH DAILY INTERACTIONS, YOU AND YOUR SPOUSE WILL INFLUENCE YOUR CHILD'S LIFE AND CONTRIBUTE TO EVERY DEVELOPMENTAL ASPECT:

WHEN YOU (AND YOUR SPOUSE):	THEN YOUR CHILD:
1. SMILE, KISS, HUG, RESPOND TO CRIES OR SIGNALS OF NEED	FEELS **EMOTIONALLY SECURE** AND SELF-CONFIDENT
2 PROVIDE NOURISHMENT, EXERCISE IN SAFE, REASSURING SURROUNDINGS	ATTAINS A **HEALTHY BODY AND PHYSICAL STRENGTH**
3. TALK, SING, READ, INTRODUCE VISUAL AND AUDITORY STIMULI	DEVELOPS **LANGUAGE**, AND OTHER **INTELLECTUAL SKILLS**
4. SHARE PLEASANT ENCOUNTERS WITH FAMILY AND FRIENDS	LEARNS TO **SOCIALIZE**, FORM RELATIONSHIPS AND **COMMUNICATE**
5. ENCOURAGE EXPLORATION OF NEW PLACES, PARTICIPATION IN NEW ACTIVITIES	BECOMES CURIOUS, **CREATIVE**, AND **WELL-ROUNDED**

1. Giving Your Baby Experiences of Warmth, Love and Connection

From the very moment your infant arrives, take pleasure in cradling your little "bundle of joy" and make your first, shared experience warm and tender. Your beautiful child is not an insensitive lump and craves your compassion and attention. Use a comforting voice, loving facial expressions, and soothing body language to communicate and welcome your son or daughter into the world. Marvel at the uniqueness of your child's little face, hands, feet, body, and voice. View your infant's impulsive, physical movements and expressive, energetic responses with amazement; your tiny infant can do so many things.

While you nourish your newborn with breast milk or formula, nurture your infant with caresses and care to lay the foundation for emotional stability, the expression of feelings, and future affectionate, social relationships.

> *Mary, an upper middle class woman in her late forties, sadly reveals that her teenage son, Tom, is asocial and drug dependent. "He was such a good baby! I don't know what happened to him," she laments. "I never had to pick him up or carry him around. I propped up his bottle in his crib at feeding time or put him in a swing most of the day and he never bothered me."*
>
> *Mary did not provide her infant with the warmth of her body or feelings of fondness. Now as a teen, he seeks comfort in addiction, not relationships.*

✳ Expressing Love to Your Baby

Surely, you want your baby to feel your affection, but how do you convey your emotions? When you and your baby share enjoyable and tender experiences, you achieve harmony and feelings of love. These warm encounters lead to a calmer home, restful nights, and pleasant dreams.

WAYS TO LOVE YOUR BABY DAY AFTER DAY

- **SMILE AND TALK TO YOUR CHILD. YOUR EXACT WORDS ARE NOT IMPORTANT. YOUR TONE OF VOICE WILL SHOW THAT YOU CARE.** When you feed your baby, simply say, "I love you, Sweetie. You're my special baby," "You're delicious."

- **CUDDLE WITH YOUR CHILD TO CONVEY YOUR AFFECTION.** When you reach into the crib each day, take your child into your arms and hug, then whisper, "Good morning. Did you have a nice night?" "Good afternoon. Did you enjoy your nap?"

📎 **KISS AND NUZZLE YOUR BABY.** When you wrap your daughter in a big towel after her bath, kiss her head, her toes, rub your nose on her belly. Your baby will love the feeling and sense your affection.

📎 **ROCK YOUR BABY IN YOUR ARMS OR IN A ROCKING CHAIR OR GLIDER.** The feeling is soothing and loving before bedtime or upon awakening.

📎 **PLAY SOFT MUSIC AS YOU GAZE INTO YOUR BABY'S EYES; SING A SONG OR HUM ALONG** while you change the diaper, clean his ears, brush his hair, and put on his clothes.

📎 **PLACE YOUR BABY ON YOUR SHOULDER AND PROVIDE A CALMING, SWAYING MOTION. GENTLY PAT OR MASSAGE YOUR BABY'S BACK, STROKE HER HAIR** and bring her comfort and love.

HELPFUL HINT:

CARING, CUDDLING, AND COMMUNICATING BRING CLOSENESS. SET AN EXAMPLE, REACH OUT TO YOUR FAMILY WITH A KIND WORD, A PAT ON THE BACK, A GENTLE TOUCH, HUG, OR KISS.

If you or your partner were not raised with open displays of affection, make a special effort to exchange kind words and snuggles at bedtime. Resolve all issues of concern before going to sleep.

❋ **Providing More Than Basic Care**

By now you have come to realize that early parent-child experiences go beyond eating, sleeping, and diaper changing. Your little baby also requires daily bathing, grooming, massaging, exercise, and preventative medical care to insure excellent, physical health. Furthermore, it is your responsibility to provide a protected, comfortable, cheerful home.

2. Helping Your Child Experience A Comforting and Safe Home Environment

Are you feeling happy and bubbly with a new baby in your life or are you down in the dumps? Is your spouse optimistic and joyful or grumpy and gloomy?

Your attitudes and emotions will affect your home environment and shape the development of your child's personality and interests; therefore, think about your inner feelings and resolve any unhappiness when you plan "priority pie" together. If the problem seems insurmountable, seek help from family, friends, or from a professional. Your goal is to enjoy your lives and provide a pleasant home for your child.

HELPFUL HINT:

FILL YOUR HOME WITH CHEERFUL PEOPLE, AND BEAUTIFUL, COMFORTING THINGS. YOUR CHILD WILL THRIVE IN A SAFE ENVIRONMENT THAT IS RICH IN LAUGHTER AND LOVE.

CREATE A HAPPY SETTING FOR YOUR GROWING CHILD:

- **INVITE FRIENDS AND FAMILY YOU ENJOY TO VISIT YOUR HOME (always consider your baby's schedule);** if you plan to have lunch or dinner, keep it casual, stress free, simply order-in and have fun socializing. Your youngster will soon learn to enjoy the company of others.

- **HANG COLORFUL PAINTINGS OR PRINTS THROUGHOUT YOUR HOME.** Pictures of trees, flowers, fruit, landscapes, etc. in the family room, bedroom, kitchen, and happy posters in the baby's room with cheerful characters and animals to stimulate visual interest and an awareness of color.

BRING THE OUTDOORS IN WITH A PRETTY PLANT OR FRESH FLOWERS ON THE TABLE; your son or daughter will learn to appreciate the beauty of nature.

DISPLAY COLORFUL PHOTOGRAPHS OF YOUR BABY IN PRETTY PICTURE FRAMES IN EVERY ROOM OF YOUR HOME; your child will soon recognize himself and feel loved.

PLACE PHOTOS OF FAMILY MEMBERS AND FRIENDS ON A SOFT MESSAGE BOARD OVER THE CHANGING TABLE. When the baby becomes more familiar with the faces, she will feel reassured to see the many people who love her.

FILL A BOX OR BOOKSHELF WITH LOTS OF ATTRAC-TIVE BOOKS made of heavy board or soft cloth. Include some musical stories. Introduce your baby to one each day and you will be surprised to find that he/she has a preference.

SHARE MUSIC BY SINGING, DANCING, LISTENING, AND HUGGING. You will stimulate the auditory senses and develop a sense of rhythm and movement. Gently rock your newborn and dance to the beat a few months later.

* **Insuring Infant Safety**

Although it is beneficial to vary your baby's environment throughout the day, your infant will require lots of sleep and will spend a great deal of time in his/her crib. Create appealing, restful surroundings for your son or daughter, with colorful, soft, cushioned bumpers, a plush toy tied tightly to the crib's sides, and a mobile secured firmly overhead. Do not forget the importance of safety.

To avoid the risk of suffocation, place your little one into the crib, on his/her back, face up, as advised by the American Academy of Pediatrics Task Force who studied SIDS (Sudden Infant Death Syndrome). A soft wedge, designed to prevent the newborn from turning, may be purchased at a children's store. Set up a video monitor to view and hear the baby when you are in another room. If you wish to use a receiving blanket for a warm and secure feeling, raise your infant's arms to allow them to move freely, wrap the torso with the blanket and tuck in the ends, papoose style, for a safe swaddle.

The American Sudden Infant Death Institute has indicated that, "belly-sleep has up to 12.9 times the risk of death as backsleep." (http://www.sids.org)

When your baby is awake and you are playing together, however, turn your child onto his/her side or stomach and place toys in view and reach. This will offer a new, interesting look at the world and prevent "Positional Plagiocephaly," flattening of the back of the head, common in back sleepers.

Do not place a blanket loosely over the baby. When your child begins to move around, remove the wedge, blankets, quilts, pillows, toys and big stuffed animals from the crib although magazines and children's stores display these items appealingly. You do not want anything to fall on your baby or cause entanglement. Be safe, drape the beautiful blanket on your rocking chair or hang the colorful quilt on a wall to add charm to the Nursery.

❋ Changing Surroundings for your Infant/Toddler

The perfect parent behaves responsibly when the baby begins to crawl and prepares a protected physical environment for safe explorations. Childproofing may include pushing a chair or table against the wall or the elimination of a piece of furniture to create a large, unobstructed, open area for movement and muscle development.

Most Moms wonder, "Can I have a beautiful home when my toddler starts to toddle? What about my porcelain collectibles or the glass bowl on my coffee table?"

Lori, eight months pregnant, argued with her Mother-in-law about removing her hand-painted boxes from a sofa side table. "I'm not changing my life for a baby!" she protested. Unfortunately, Lori needed a wake-up call, but not from her Mother-in-law.

As an adult and a parent, you need to realize that your baby will not understand the value of your possessions. Furthermore, anything breakable can be dangerous for the child. Preserve your special pieces in a curio box, in an armoire, or place them out of reach on a high shelf, and one day you can share your collection with your son or daughter. Accessorize your home with soft pillows and unbreakable artifacts for warmth and charm.

As an inexperienced Mother, I kept my crystal candlesticks on a low, display shelf. When my son began to walk and reach from one piece of furniture to another to gain balance and confidence, I called out, "Be careful! Don't touch Mommy's favorite candlesticks!"

*Did a curious one year old know the meaning of 'candlesticks' or 'careful?' It was almost instantaneous. He reached for the étagère; the glass fell to the ground and frightened us both. As I swept up the broken pieces, I felt lucky that he wasn't hurt and I learned that **A PARENT MUST MAKE IT EASY FOR A CHILD TO BE SAFE AND WELL-BEHAVED.***

HELPFUL HINT:

CREATE A CHILD-FRIENDLY ENVIRONMENT IN YOUR HOME BY REMOVING POTENTIALLY BREAKABLE OR HAZARDOUS OBJECTS AND PLACING CHERISHED POSSESSIONS OUT OF YOUR CHILD'S REACH.

CHILD-PROOF YOUR HOME

Building supply stores and shops where baby necessities are sold carry items to promote home safety. Since prices vary, try some comparison-shopping and your own creativity.

- Cover all electrical outlets.

- Place electrical cords, poisons (like pesticides, kerosene, lighter fluid, cleaning solutions, detergents, drain cleaner, medicine, etc.) or sharp items, glass bottles, pottery, and other breakables out of reach or in locked cabinets. (Your curious, little one will surely find every "unsafe" object and cupboard filled with hazardous or fragile items in your home.)

- Remove furniture with rough edges, or pointed, sharp corners, or cover the hazardous parts with rubber or foam. (Check in 'plumbing supplies' for inexpensive "self seal pipe insulation" that can work around most table edges.)

- Keep cribs and beds away from dangling cords on window blinds; tie them up, out of reach.

- Install gates at the top and bottom of stairs and keep them closed.

- Repair chipped wooden floors and sand any furniture with splintered edges.

- Place appropriate "stops" at doors and drawers to prevent fingers from getting caught. Kids love the idea of "opening and shutting" and do not realize the danger of placing their fingers near the hinges or between the door or drawer and the frame.

- Cover oven knobs.

✤ Shut doors to bathrooms and rooms with exercise equipment; fingers can get injured under a treadmill, between gears, under weights.

✤ When decorating your home with plants, check with the gardening store regarding poisonous ones. For example, avoid dieffenbachia, poinsettia, and philodendron.

✤ Create an open space for movement, exercise, dance, and play. Enjoy healthy fun with your child and tone your own body at the same time.

HELPFUL HINT:

WHEN YOUR CHILD BEGINS TO MOVE AROUND THE HOUSE, HE WILL TRY TO OPEN EVERY CABINET, SO BE PREPARED. SET ONE LOWER UNIT ASIDE IN THE KITCHEN JUST FOR HIM. REMOVE YOUR BELONGINGS AND FILL IT UP WITH TOYS, SMALL EMPTY BOXES, UNBREAKABLE BOWLS, CUPS, OR POTS AND EXPLAIN, "THIS IS YOUR SPECIAL CUBBY AND YOU CAN HELP MOMMY AND DADDY WORK IN THE KITCHEN."

✳ **Creating Room Changes with Your Young Child (2 - 3 years and over)**

As a child grows, room requirements change as well, but comfort and safety are always important considerations. If you designed a "baby area" two - three years ago, your tot may be ready to move from a crib to a bed and need more "floor space" to play or entertain friends. Active children and sharp furniture edges signal "accidents waiting to happen." Do not depend on furniture designers to protect your son or daughter. Look for rounded edges and consider a plush carpet in place of a wood or tiled floor.

As your toddler grows, you will notice that he/she is forming a distinctive personality with special preferences. ***Encourage your child to make choices, but guide these opinions and consider what is in his/her best interest.***

Rachel and Pete were expecting their second child and took Billy, two-and-a-half years old, to buy a "big boy" bed. Billy immediately pointed to the high bunk bed and ladder, attractively set with a big red, fluffy dog.

Realizing that her son was too young to climb in and out safely, Rachel reached up, grabbed the stuffed toy and placed it on a low youth bed. "Which one do you like?" she asked and Billy responded as expected. "Want bed with doggy!" "Great choice, Billy!" smiled his Dad.

When you share the experience of creating new surroundings with your youngster, direct the selections by offering alternatives:

"Would you like a yellow room or a blue one? Should we paint Mickey Mouse or Snoopy on your walls? Would you like to put your stuffed animals on a shelf or in a toy box?"

WHEN YOU ASK YOUR CHILD TO MAKE A CHOICE, YOU TEACH THE IMPORTANCE OF ORGANIZING AND DECISION-MAKING. WHEN YOU LISTEN TO THE SUGGESTION, YOU CONVEY A SENSE OF HIS/HER IMPORTANCE AND YOU HELP TO CONNECT YOUR SON OR DAUGHTER TO YOUR HOME AND FAMILY. IF YOU ARE NON-JUDGMENTAL, YOU INSURE A FUTURE OF OPEN COMMUNICATION.

HELPFUL HINTS:

WHEN A NEW SIBLING IS ON THE WAY AND AN ENVIRONMENTAL CHANGE IS NECESSARY FOR THE "BIG BROTHER OR SISTER":

❖ **MAKE THE ADJUSTMENT LONG BEFORE THE INFANT ARRIVES (2-3 MONTHS IN ADVANCE WILL EASE THE TRANSITION)**

❖ **INVOLVE YOUR OLDER CHILD IN THE PLANS AND CHOICES AND SPEAK OF HIS/HER IMPORTANCE IN HELPING**

❖ **GIVE LOTS OF HUGS, KISSES, AND REASSURANCES THAT YOU LOVE HIM/HER VERY MUCH WHENEVER YOU TALK ABOUT THE NEW BABY**

As a compassionate parent who considers the well being of her child first, you will aim to develop a warm, safe environment, filled with emotional nurturing and healthy basic care; you are, however, also responsible for providing experiences of mental stimulation and communication.

3. Stimulating Intellectual Experiences and Communication

Many parents wonder, "When does learning begin? Should I wait for the Nursery School teacher to talk about colors, letters, and numbers? If I teach my child too many things, won't he be bored in school?"

Put those questions aside and provide as many learning experiences as you can, from infancy onward. If you motivate your child early in life to look, listen, think, and discover, you will increase curiosity and the desire to learn more.

HELPFUL HINT:

YOU CAN INSPIRE AND MOLD YOUR INFANT'S SCHOLARLY AND COMMUNICATIVE ABILITIES FROM THE VERY START; INTRODUCE THE SIGHTS, SOUNDS, TASTES, AND SENSATIONS OF OUR WORLD AND EXPAND ATTENTIVENESS, LANGUAGE, KNOWLEDGE, AND BRAINPOWER.

✳ **Motivating the Visual and Auditory Senses**

The movement of an overhead, colorful, musical mobile will not only engage the eyes and the ears, but also stimulate reaching and stretching. Firmly attach the toy to the crib's side to hang above, but slightly in front of the infant and when the child awakens, he/she will enjoy the sights and the sounds.

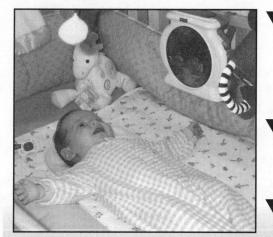

BRING OUT BABY'S SMILES WITH MOVING, MUSICAL CRIB TOYS.

▼ Tie a "PATTERNED" toy onto the crib, in your son or daughter's view. Choose dots, stripes, or checks.

▼ A toy with "MOTION AND MUSIC" is exciting for the baby, too.

▼ Secure a toy that is "REFLEC-TIVE," mirror-like," (with cushioned edges) to the opposite side of the crib. When the infant turns and smiles, self-discovery begins.

Since your little one's attention span is short, whenever he/she is awake inspire visual skills: vary activities, change body positions, and relocate your baby to new places. Stay with your infant as you turn her sideways or onto her stomach; your facial features and the environmental sights will become familiar.

Wind a music box, play a musical tape/CD, hold your baby in your lap and gently tap a toy piano or drum, read a musical book, and arouse your child's listening skills. Your closeness and communicative sounds will be reassuring.

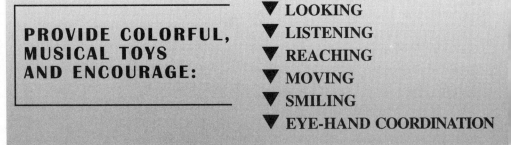

PROVIDE COLORFUL, MUSICAL TOYS AND ENCOURAGE:

▼ LOOKING
▼ LISTENING
▼ REACHING
▼ MOVING
▼ SMILING
▼ EYE-HAND COORDINATION

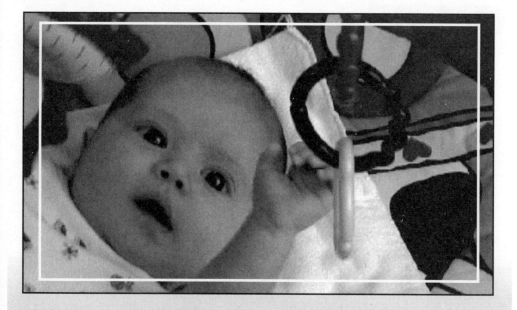

- ▼ A MELODIC MOBILE
- ▼ A SERIES OF RINGS
- ▼ SHORT, WIGGLY STREAMERS OVERHEAD
- ▼ SOFT RATTLES TO SHAKE
- ▼ SAFE TOYS TO TASTE

PRESENT ONLY ONE INTERESTING TOY AT A TIME, BUT OFFER A VARIETY DURING THE DAY:

YOUR BABY'S FIRST MOVEMENTS WILL BE

THRILLING. CAPTURE IT ALL ON VIDEO

AND YOU WILL ENJOY

SEEING THOSE MOMENTS AGAIN AND AGAIN.

HELPFUL HINT:

TO DEVELOP AN ACTIVE, HEALTHY BABY FROM THE START, CHANGE POSITIONS, OUTLOOKS, ACTIVITIES, AND COMMUNICATE:

❖ **EXPLORE YOUR HOME: It is early morning. You have washed, changed and fed your infant. Now cuddle your child in your arms and speak softly as you walk around your apartment or house.**

> *Talk about anything and everything, the lights overhead or the spinning fan in the family room, the sounds of the ticking clock in the hall, or the water running from the kitchen faucet, the lingering smell of your spouse's cologne. Sit on the living room sofa and admire the flowers in the painting on the wall, or rock in a chair in the nursery and sing a song. Your motion or cuddling, the sound of your voice, even your smell will be calming before the morning nap.*

❖ **TOUR YOUR NEIGHBORHOOD: When your baby's morning nap is over, it may be time to change, feed, and burp her again. Then dress her in accordance with the weather, place her in a stroller, walk around the neighborhood and describe your surroundings.**

> *"It's cool today, or hot, or windy, the yellow sun is shining, the sky is blue. See the birds, the tall, green trees." Talk, talk, talk while the motion of the stroller soothes with gentle movement. Although, your newborn won't understand the conversation in the beginning, you will get in the habit of communicating with your child and in a few months, your baby will sit up and notice the trees or the sun when you walk outdoors. It may be only several months later when your son or daughter tries to repeat your words, to your amazement. By 18-24 months, you will enjoy the start of verbal interaction.*

❖ **SEE THE WORLD FROM A "BOUNCY" SEAT:** When your baby is able to sit in a reclining chair or infant seat, allow him to view a children's musical video (no more than ten minutes) and sing along, or place yourself or your spouse in view of the baby when you work. Give your baby a small rattle or toy to shake.

Your little one will enjoy watching you cook, dust, place pictures in an album, or simply relax. It is nice to spend "awake" time together and have a little chat.

❖ **DISCOVER COLORS, MOVEMENT AND SOUNDS:** In a bright area in your home, carefully lay your baby on a fanciful, children's quilt, or a pad and blanket, on the floor, face up to develop the senses.

Your infant will wave his arms and move his legs excitedly.

❖ **ENCOURAGE SCOOTING AND CRAWLING:** When your son or daughter is six or seven months old and can turn and sit up, place her on her tummy, on a quilt, with a toy in front of her, in full view.

Your baby will stretch and move forward to reach the object.

HELPFUL HINT:

WHEN YOU PLAY WITH AN INFANT OR TODDLER, "LESS IS MORE."

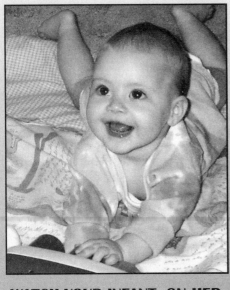

WATCH YOUR INFANT, ON HER TUMMY, REACH FOR A TOY AND SCOOT FORWARD.

▼ **DO NOT CONFUSE, DISTRACT, OR OVERWHELM YOUR CHILD WITH TOO MANY 'EDUCATIONAL' TOYS AT ONCE.**

▼ **PERMIT YOUR BABY TO FOCUS AND EXPLORE ONE OBJECT AT A TIME. WHEN YOUR CHILD LOSES INTEREST, REMOVE IT AND PRESENT ANOTHER TOY.**

▼ **REINTRODUCE THE FIRST TOY ON ANOTHER DAY AND IT WILL SEEM FRESH AND NEW.**

As you aim to provide the most enriching experiences, remember that **"MECHANICAL BABYSITTERS"** cannot replace necessary, caring contact. If you place your child in a **MUSICAL SWING** or in a **JUMPING DEVICE** for more than 15 minutes at a time, you are depriving your infant of your warmth and love. Of course, it is important to give your baby some independent playtime for discovery and creativity, but the loving environment of parent-child communicative experiences are priceless.

Your whispers, laughter, your spouse's voice, soft lullabies, tunes in musical books, music boxes, and wind-up toys will calm your baby and eliminate feelings of isolation. These sounds will also prompt your infant to vocalize; this is important for the beginning of speech.

You are your child's first social contact, so be sure to smile, gurgle, and your baby will smile and gurgle again and again.

HAVE A LITTLE CHAT WITH YOUR BABY AND INSPIRE LANGUAGE DEVELOPMENT

Share face-to-face time, talking, listening, smiling, singing, laughing, hugging, and kissing. Your child will develop language, facial expressions, a full range of emotions, and a loving bond.

WHENEVER YOU ARE NEAR YOUR BABY, DURING FEEDING, CHANGING, BATHING, OR PLAYING, TALK TO YOUR INFANT AS IF HE UNDERSTANDS EVERY SPOKEN SYLLABLE; KIDS COMPREHEND BEFORE THEY CAN EXPRESS THEMSELVES. YOUR VOICE, EYE CONTACT, AND INTONATION WILL STIMULATE INTEREST IN VERBAL COMMUNICATION.

As your schedule permits each morning and evening, lie down with your infant, or sit on the floor with your toddler, with a quilt or blanket beneath you both. If you work, you may need to awaken 15 minutes earlier than usual for your morning playtime. Plan for 10 - 15 minutes of play activities when you return from work, as well. Include your spouse in the fun, too. Discuss the agenda in advance to allow both parents to participate individually or as a team. Preparation is an important part of 'perfect' parenting.

RESERVE 10-15 MINUTES, TWICE A DAY, FOR "QUALITY" PLAYTIME WITH YOUR BABY

- **PLAY PEEK-A-BOO** behind a blanket or hide behind a chair and reappear.
- **WIGGLE A PUPPET AND SING A SONG** to get the giggles going.
- **WIND UP A MUSICAL TOY** and clap your hands with the beat.
- **SHAKE A RATTLE OR A TAMBOURINE, TAP A DRUM** and watch the response.
- **BLOW BUBBLES UP HIGH INTO THE AIR** to encourage looking, grasping, and eye-hand coordination. (Begin at 5 - 6 months.) This is fun in the bath, too.
- **STACK BLOCKS AND KNOCK THEM DOWN.** Pile them again (Start with three blocks at 6 - 9 months) and encourage your little boy or girl to do the same.   Make the tower higher and higher for your toddler.
- **OPEN AND SHUT THE DOORS ON A BUSY BOX;** then allow your older infant or toddler to explore on his own.
- **INTRODUCE A VARIETY OF BOOKS,** as soon as your infant will look and focus, turn the pages of a cloth or board book, press the buttons on a musical book, and before long your daughter will "read" on her own.

HELPFUL HINTS:

TO KEEP PLAYTIME INNOVATIVE:

❖ USE YOUR CHILD'S TOYS, STORIES, AND MUSIC TO INSPIRE THE "QUALITY TIME" YOU SHARE

❖ ROTATE NEW, AGE-APPROPRIATE PLAYTHINGS IN THE CAR SEAT, STROLLER, PLAYPEN, AND ON THE HIGH CHAIR TRAY EACH WEEK

❊   **Providing "Input" to Receive "Output"**

Since you are most important in your child's life, your responsiveness and "input" will have a lasting effect on your youngster. However, if like most parents, you are actively engaged in work activities, social events, personal projects, and always busy on the phone, the computer, reading, or watching TV, you will deprive your child of your full attention. Doesn't your youngster deserve to feel special?

MAKE EVERY EFFORT TO GIVE YOUR GROWING CHILD YOUR TOTAL CONSIDERATION AND EXPERIENCES THAT ARE ENRICHING; YOU CAN PROVIDE "QUALITY" IN-PUT:

▼ **MAKE A CONSCIOUS ATTEMPT TO INTERACT WITH YOUR CHILD WITH-OUT BEING DISTRACTED: SIT ON THE FLOOR, FACE-TO-FACE, ENGAGE IN EYE CONTACT AND CONVER-SATION** (You may be the only one talking), **AND ALLOW YOUR BABY TO SEE YOUR SMILE, HEAR YOUR VOICE, FEEL YOUR TOUCH.**

▼ **BE PATIENT, ENERGETIC** (Sleep when your baby does and recharge), **AND EXPLORE A CHALLENGING AND AGE-APPROPRIATE ACTIVITY WITH YOUR SON OR DAUGHTER.**

▼ **ALWAYS SAY, "I'M PROUD OF YOU. GREAT TRY! GREAT JOB!"** (Your infant will sense your happiness and your toddler will feel motivated.)

▼ **DO NOT WAIT FOR YOUR BABY TO SEEK ATTENTION. INITIATE PLAY, CONVERSA-TION, HUGS, KISSES.** (A child who feels neglected will do annoying things just to get noticed.)

REMOVING THE RINGS WAS EASY, BUT GETTING THEM BACK ON WILL TAKE LOTS OF TRIES.

HELP YOUR YOUNGSTER FACE THE WORLD CONFIDENT-LY, INDEPENDENTLY, YET SECURE IN THE FACT THAT YOUR SUPPORT AND LOVE IS ALWAYS AVAILABLE. If there is more than one child in your home, divide your time between them. "Now it's Austin's special time with Mommy. We'll set the timer for 15 minutes and then it will be Madeline's 15 minutes. After her turn, we will all play together.

HELPFUL HINT:

YOUR QUALITY "IN-PUT"= YOUR CHILD'S SUCCESSFUL "OUTPUT."

How can you raise the "total child," one who is well rounded, knowledgeable, and skilled in many areas? Begin early and introduce your infant, than your toddler, and pre-school child to a wide spectrum of activities.

SHARE A VARIETY OF FUN-FILLED EXPERIENCES WITH YOUR TODDLER AND PRE-SCHOOLER (IN-PUT) TO ENHANCE EMOTIONAL, SOCIAL, INTELLECTUAL, CREATIVE, AND PHYSICAL DEVELOPMENT (OUT-PUT):

❖ **MOVE TO THE MUSIC, SING, AND DANCE,** as you share in rhythmic, musical and movement interplays.

❖ **SHARE ARTISTIC ACTIVITIES,** such as coloring, painting, modeling clay.

❖ **PLAY WITH PUZZLES, BUILD A TOWER, THROW A BALL, DRAMATIZE WITH DOLLS OR PUPPETS** and your child will love your interaction.

BRING OUT THE SPOONS, MIXERS, SPREADERS, PANS, as your youngster joins you in the kitchen to mix, spread, cook or bake. Include your spouse in the fun to help your child stir and spread.

EXPLORE DAYTIME TOGETHER AND UNCOVER THE WONDERS OF NATURE, the sun, the clouds, the birds, spiders, animals, the beach, etc.

WATER THE FLOWERS TOGETHER, OR PLANT A GARDEN, and your child will learn to cooperate and care about plants and other living things.

LOOK UP AT THE NIGHT SKY with your son or daughter to rediscover the darkness, the moon and stars; respond to your child's interests and inquisitiveness.

ENJOY NEW EXHILARATION ON A BUS OR TRAIN RIDE, A TRIP BY PLANE OR SHIP and try to answer all the questions your child asks.

GAIN A NEW PERSPECTIVE IN THE MALL, PET SHOP, ZOO, CIRCUS, MOVIES, THEATER, MUSEUM, LIBRARY, RODEO, RESTAURANT, MARKET, etc. Choose activities based on your child's readiness and your patience.

As an involved and loving parent, you lay the foundation for emotional strength, academic development, and social behavior in the very early years of your child's life.

4. ENJOYING SOCIAL EXPERIENCES

You can set the climate for active socialization if you first encourage your son or daughter to participate in a variety of exchanges with relatives and close friends in your own home. Arrange many visits to and from familiar faces, in a safe environment that will allow your youngster to feel confident and comfortable. Before long, your child will feel open to meeting new people in new places, without fear or hesitation, and with socially acceptable behavior.

❋   **Sharing Meals At Home**

WHEN EVERYONE IN THE FAMILY SHARES A MEAL THERE IS MUCH TO BE GAINED. EVEN A VERY YOUNG CHILD LOOKS FORWARD TO THAT PREDICTABLE, SPECIAL TIME TOGETHER.

Your child will learn to interact with a group and acquire the skills of conversation, communication, and socialization. As your child grows, he will find security in knowing that there's a place to discuss the day's activities, exchange ideas, opinions, plans, and seek advice. A shared dinner is usually best, but if a family member works late or is involved with late classes, try to enjoy breakfast, a mutual snack, dessert, or Sunday brunch. In years to come you will remain connected to your growing son or daughter.

Whether your family is a traditional 'Mom, Dad and child' configuration, or a newly accepted 21st century arrangement, **EVERY PERSON FEELS INCLUDED, COMFORTED, AND STABLIZED WITH DAILY, FAMILY TABLE TALK.** These experiences are unmatched.

HELPFUL HINT:

WHEN YOU SHARE MEALS IN YOUR HOME, IN RESTAURANTS, OR ATTEND OTHER SOCIAL EVENTS WITH YOUR CHILD, YOU AND YOUR SPOUSE SET THE EXAMPLES FOR ACCEPTABLE SOCIAL CONDUCT.

✳ Sharing Meals in Restaurants

Some parents, unfortunately, do not include their children in the experience of dining out. They exclude their kids from the social scene and fail to introduce them to worldly sights. Who misses out? Both the parents and the kids!

> *For example, Julie never prepared her sons for social settings and admits, "I didn't take them to restaurants when they were little because I was afraid they would act like animals. Now at ages 4, 7, and 9, they do act like animals. My husband works evenings, grabs fast food while I microwave frozen dinners for myself. The kids eat chicken sticks, peanut butter, cheese, or bologna sandwiches in the family room while watching TV and on weekends we get a sitter and escape!"*

> *Although most parents experience life with their children and help them learn proper societal behavior, Julie and her husband did not provide the necessary role models or the experiences. Their boys, therefore, never learned to wash before eating, were not familiar with healthy food choices, never used proper eating utensils, and never learned to speak pleasantly at the dinner table.*

TO ENJOY A FAMILY OUTING, PLAN AHEAD, CONSIDER YOUR CHILD'S EATING/SLEEPING ROUTINES, LIKES, DISLIKES, PATIENCE LEVEL, & TEMPERAMENT.

THIS YOUNG TODDLER IS PREPARED TO ENJOY CONVERSATION AND DINNER WITH HIS FAMILY IN A "CHILD-FRIENDLY" RESTAURANT WHERE HIS FAVORITE FOODS ARE AVAILABLE.

HIS PARENTS HAVE COME PREPARED WITH A COLORFUL PLACEMAT, BOOKS, CRAYONS, AND A SMALL, QUIET TOY.

RULES FOR DINING OUT

1   Plan to eat during your youngster's regular mealtime schedule.

2.   Eat at a child-friendly restaurant and check the menu before going to the table to find something that your little one will enjoy.

3.   Consider the "waiting time," order your food, and take a short walk outside the restaurant or a trip to the bathroom to wash.

4.   Always come prepared with a bag of toys, cards, crayons, and books to distract and teach. Have a small snack available, too, but do not bring it out unless the wait is longer than anticipated.

5.   If you have played with everything, count the sugars, spoons, and straws. Look at pictures on the menu or discuss the artwork hanging in the room, or the designs or lights on the walls and ceilings.

6.   Remember to praise your child, "I'm so proud of you when you sit and speak quietly in a restaurant. You are a big boy."

From the time Jonathan was a baby, Sara encouraged her son to meet new people, visit new places, and share dining experiences. This four year old enjoyed socializing, but his mother knew his limitations. When her in-laws visited for lunch, she selected a suitable neighborhood eatery. "We are going to have lunch with Grandma and Grandpa today," she told Jon excitedly. "You may choose a yummy grilled cheese sandwich or spaghetti and meatballs." Sara offered two menu options in advance. "Which do you think you might choose?" If Jonathan had responded, "I want chicken nuggets at the Burger restaurant," she would have calmly retorted, "It will be your turn to choose a place to eat on Sunday, but it's my turn today. We're all going to have a great time."

Before going out, Sara asks Jon, "Would you like to bring this story or your small car, crayons and a page to color or a deck of cards?" She allows him to choose from the "small, quiet items" she has selected and includes a few surprises in her bag. She also reminds her son not to run in the restaurant and disturb others. "If it takes a long time until the food arrives, you may have two crackers or the cup of fruit we are bringing and then we'll show Grandma and Grandpa some of your toys or books. I know you will make us all feel proud of you."

HELPFUL HINT:

WHEN PREPARING FOR SOCIAL SITUATIONS, HELP YOUR CHILD KNOW "WHAT TO EXPECT" AND "WHAT IS EXPECTED" OF HIM. THE RULES YOU PUT INTO EFFECT AT AN EARLY AGE DETERMINE FUTURE BEHAVIOR.

If your two-year-old daughter has a tantrum at the restaurant table mid-meal, immediately remove her from the scene and let her calm down. Then try again, "Let's finish our lunch like a big girl." If it seems that she cannot handle the day and cries again, ask for your food to be wrapped and leave. It may be embarrassing if you are with others, but to have your child continue to act inappropriately at the table and ruin everyone's meal would be unfair. Furthermore, it is best to set your standards early; to have your child display tantrum behavior at age eight would surely be more humiliating.

✳ Sharing Meals At Home

IF YOU CONSIDER YOUR CHILD'S AGE, READINESS, INTERESTS, AND TASTES WHEN YOU MAKE PLANS, YOU WILL MAKE IT EASIER FOR YOUR YOUNGSTER TO "DO THE RIGHT THING." Have you ever felt jealous of a friend or family member whose child is always well behaved? Is this luck or better parenting?

Sean and Hannah, both thirteen months old, loved to play side by side when their mothers planned play dates. This week, they tried lunch. Charlotte prepared macaroni and cheese and placed two plastic bowls with fresh berries on the table. "Pasta and berries are Sean's favorites," Charlotte told her friend, Marilyn, as her son happily devoured his lunch. "I hope Hannah likes it, too."

Marilyn took two jars from her bag, squash and ground chicken, and attempted to feed Hannah, but the baby cried, spit out the strained food and pushed it away. Marilyn was upset. "Hannah never eats. She's terrible and Sean is so good."

Charlotte was taken aback, but calmly handed her friend a plate of mac and cheese and a bowl of berries. "Why don't you try real food? Once Sean's teeth came in, he pushed away his baby food, too. Even babies have likes and dislikes."

Marilyn felt embarrassed and offered Hannah the pasta and berries, as her friend suggested. The little girl loved feeding herself and Marilyn realized Sean's behavior was great because his mother was "tuned-in" to his readiness and was sensitive to his tastes. Charlotte was "in-sync" with her son and made it easy for him to cooperate.

HELPFUL HINT:

IF YOU ARE A FLEXIBLE AND ADAPTIVE PARENT, SENSITIVE TO YOUR CHILD'S FEELINGS AND READINESS, YOU WILL HAVE A MORE COOPERATIVE AND EMOTIONALLY HEALTHY YOUNGSTER.

Use discretion when introducing your child to new foods, novel experiences and unfamiliar events both in and out of the home. If you suspect that your youngster will be unable to enjoy an activity, a visit to the planetarium, a music concert, an evening party, the State Fair, etc., do not go. If you anticipate stress, unhappiness, lack of readiness or appropriateness avoid that situation for your child, for you, and for others in attendance.

> *Holly and Paul were excited about the Smiths' Christmas Party. When their sitter canceled an hour before the event, they decided to take their five year old to this evening affair even though it coincided with their son's bedtime. Little Doug inevitably dropped chips and salsa on their neighbor's imported rug only minutes after their arrival. Then the double-dipping adventure began! Doug dipped carrot sticks into the onion dip, licked and dipped again into the salsa, licked his fingers, dipped again! The other guests were appalled at the couple's lack of parental control, but Holly and Paul neither concerned themselves with the party guests, nor their child. Doug never learned a social skill from the experience. They finally left at 10 p.m. after the little boy's tantrum.*

✳ Correcting Unacceptable Social Behavior

CHARACTER AND VALUES DEVELOP EARLY AS YOUR TOT EXPERIENCES LIFE WITH YOU, SO BE FIRM FROM THE BEGINNING, SET RULES, LIMITS, TRY TO BUILD PLEASING QUALITIES, AND PRESENT A PARENTAL UNITED FRONT. If Mom says, "No! You can't have that toy," but Dad buys it, the child learns to manipulate the 'easy' parent and create marital disagreements.

If you permit your two year old to musically hit your drinking glasses with a spoon at home, he will do the same with your mother-in-law's fine sterling and crystal. The value of the table setting is not his concern. Your Mother-in-law will remind you, of course, that her children never did that!

If your child always eats alone in the kitchen or marches around the house with tidbits, he will do the same thing during Thanksgiving dinner although the entire family is seated together for the turkey carving. If you expect your youngster to sit quietly at the dining room table for the very first time to wait for the fowl, you can be sure that your child's mood will be foul.

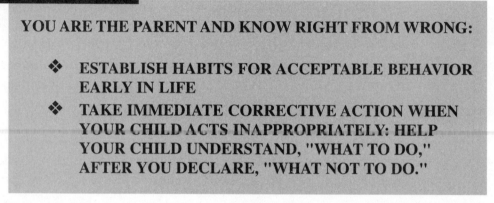

HELPFUL HINTS:

YOU ARE THE PARENT AND KNOW RIGHT FROM WRONG:

❖ **ESTABLISH HABITS FOR ACCEPTABLE BEHAVIOR EARLY IN LIFE**

❖ **TAKE IMMEDIATE CORRECTIVE ACTION WHEN YOUR CHILD ACTS INAPPROPRIATELY: HELP YOUR CHILD UNDERSTAND, "WHAT TO DO," AFTER YOU DECLARE, "WHAT NOT TO DO."**

Don't fool yourself into thinking that irritating conduct will vanish by itself. Infuriating behavior usually continues into an exaggerated form as your child ages.

> *Michael was a bright little boy who realized, at age two and a half, that he could control Mom and Dad by shouting his demands in public and embarrassing them. When it was close to dinnertime and Mom refused to buy candy in the mall, Michael screamed until she did. At age six, he threw a tantrum in the toy store until his father bought the electronic game he wanted. At age fifteen, both parents conceded and purchased the expensive computer he demanded in his shrill voice. At twenty-eight, his wife now addresses these troublesome tantrums and resents her in-laws for creating an "obnoxious, spoiled brat!"*

If you are not tuned-in to your child's feelings and have difficulty understanding her language, it is logical that she will be frustrated and angry. Wouldn't you be upset if your spouse didn't pay attention to your comments and wishes?

The "tantrum experience" is always exasperating for everyone. Therefore, try to be "in-sync" with your child's needs and you may be able to intercept a tantrum before it begins. Distraction and reasoning are good devices, but once the screaming has become uncontrollable and the thrashing has begun, nothing will work. Carry your screaming son or daughter away from the situation, to a carpeted or cushioned, "safe" place, when possible. In time, your youngster will calm down and the anger will pass. Rub your child's back, hug, kiss, and remind him, "I'm always proud of you when you speak like a big boy. If you tell me what you want, I will try to understand you, but when you cry and scream it hurts my ears and I cannot hear anything you are trying to say." The child learns that screaming and tantrums do not pay.

> **TODDLER TANTRUMS**
>
> **ARE TYPICAL AS CHILDREN BECOME INCREASINGLY INDEPENDENT AND OPINIONATED, BUT OFTEN UNABLE TO EXPRESS THEMSELVES.**

5. SELECTING CAREGIVERS WHO CAN PROVIDE QUALITY EXPERIENCES

If you are a busy parent, actively striving towards success in all you do and feeling anxious because you cannot always be there for your son or daughter, you may also be concerned about the Nanny or the Day Care Center worker that you have chosen. Will this individual adequately substitute for you and provide the care you and your spouse value?

Who will experience life with your child when you cannot? Who will watch your baby take the first step, say the first word, and smell the first flower? Who will attend dancing school, soccer practice, or the school play? Can you avoid feelings of guilt when you leave your baby and miss those joyous moments and milestones?

IF YOU ARE A WORKING PARENT, YOU CAN REDUCE YOUR ANXIETY:

- **SIMPLY SHARE AFFECTIONATE, PARENT-CHILD "TOGETHER TIME," EACH MORNING AND EVENING AND FEEL CONFIDENT THAT THESE MOMENTS OF "GIVING YOUR BEST" ARE INVALUABLE.** Often non-working parents provide less attentive interactions than parents who work.

- **FIND A DEPENDABLE, NURTURING CAREGIVER WITH A PHILOSOPHY THAT IS CONSISTENT WITH YOUR THOUGHTS AND BELIEFS.** Start your search early, so you are not desperately seeking help the day before work begins.

Children become confused when they are raised by a series of inconsistent people. They do not have a clear understanding of how to act, react, or how to please an adult.

ONE STABLE CARE-GIVER BUILDS TRUST, SECURITY, CONSISTENCY AND LOVE.

A CHILD WHO IS RAISED BY MANY CAREGIVERS WITH VARIED STYLES AND PERSONALITIES FEELS LIKE A YOUNGSTER WHO IS RAISED BY A SCHIZOPHRENIC PARENT WITH MOOD SWINGS.

NARROW THE NANNY SEARCH

❋ Select your Nanny carefully through **interviews, verified references, and several trial days** before leaving your baby alone with this stranger. Watch her interactions with the little one. Does she handle your child the way you do?

❋ Ask for proof of **past experience, education, and CPR/First Aid training**. If she is well skilled, she may teach you a few good techniques.

❋ If you find your Nanny **on the internet, be safe:** schedule an interview out of your home, without your child, until you do **criminal and Social Security background checks.**

❋ Does she seem **warm, encouraging, gentle, and speak well?**

❋ Does she appear **clean and wash her hands** before touching your infant when she arrives? She will later convey her habits of cleanliness to your growing son or daughter.

❋ Does she seem to be **organized?** You do not want a Nanny who is late, forgetful, or unreliable.

❋ Is she **respectful of your wishes and instructions?** On a trial day, give her a reasonable list of things to do (wash bottles, hand wash laundry) and see her level of cooperation.

❋ Will she play, sing and offer **intellectual stimulation**, take the baby for walks, or simply feed, change, and pacify?

❋ When you feel comfortable, leave for an hour, then three hours, and finally for a full day. **Does your child seem well cared for and happy when you return?**

Ali resigned from her job when Mason was born because her traditional husband, Josh, believed that a mother should be home with her child. Ali agreed in theory, but Mason's true Caregiver was their non-English speaking, Venezuelan housekeeper who was more involved with cleaning and cooking than with Mason. Grandma visited twice a week to take him out for treats and toys. A teen came in to help on Saturdays. Ali had a busy schedule of shopping, exercising, beauty activities, and lunches with friends while Mason was ignored by one Caregiver, over-indulged by Grandma, and often reprimanded by the young sitter.

During his second birthday party, Ali and Josh compared their son to the other kids and noticed his lack of speech and cooperative conduct. Sadly, Mason was confused because each Caregiver expected different behavior from him and one didn't even speak the same language. This little boy lacked consistency and parental quality time.

Whether you are a stay-at-home parent or work outside the house, discuss your values, morals, goals, and behavioral expectations with your loved one and pass them on to one Caregiver who understands you and your child. In addition, discuss your feelings about childrearing with your parents, in-laws, and other family members who come in contact with your child frequently. Try to establish mutual understandings. "We all want the best for Tyler. He's our first priority."

Tyler, two and a half years old, loved the big, sticky, sugary lollipops his grandma brought for him each week when she visited, but his parents preferred healthier snacks. Tyler's Dad did not want to insult his mother, but he called her and diplomatically said, "Mom, it's so nice of you to always bring Tyler a treat. Would you mind picking up some berries for him when you come tomorrow? He loves fruit and since he can't brush his teeth well, we would prefer that to candy." The message was clear, not confrontational.

During your child's growing years, family, friends, teachers, care-givers, and people in the media will communicate various beliefs and atti-tudes to influence your son or daughter's thoughts and behavior. However, your love, concern, and the quality time you provide as you **EXPERI-ENCE LIFE TOGETHER, "E,"** will have the most important impact.

HELPFUL HINT:

YOU CAN HELP YOUR SON OR DAUGHTER REACH SUCCESS:

❖ **PROVIDE LOVE, CARE, ATTENTION, AND UNDER STANDING**

❖ **EXPERIENCE LIFE TOGETHER ("IN-PUT") AND STIMULATE DEVELOPMENT ("OUT-PUT")**

Highlights

"E"= EXPERIENCE LIFE WITH YOUR CHILD FROM INFANCY ONWARD, AND DEVELOP A WELL-ROUNDED, SUCCESSFUL INDIVIDUAL.

1. YOU ARE THE MOST IMPORTANT INFLUENCE IN YOUR CHILD'S LIFE AND CONTRIBUTE TO EVERY DEVELOP MENTAL ASPECT:
    - *Give your baby daily "EMOTIONAL EXPERIENCES" of warmth, love, security, and connection, beyond basic care.*
    - *Create a happy, comfortable, safe home environment with PHYSICAL EXPERIENCES" of nourishment and exercise.*
    - *Encourage "INTELLECTUAL EXPERIENCES," the discovery of colors, movement, music, and language*
    - *Prepare your child for "SOCIAL EXPERIENCES" and responsibilities by communicating "what to expect" and "what is expected of him."*

2. MAKE IT EASY FOR YOUR CHILD TO "DO THE RIGHT THING:
    - *Respond to readiness, needs, age, and select appropriate activities.*
    - *Establish consistent, acceptable, behavior.*
    - *"DISTRACT AND SUBSTITUTE" to change behavior.*

3. SELECT ONE CAREGIVER WHO FOLLOWS YOUR GUIDE LINES and is able to impart first-rate experiences.

4. DEVELOP THE BEST IN YOUR CHILD WITH YOUR ATTENTION, LOVE, AND "QUALITY TIME:" YOUR "IN-PUT"= YOUR YOUNGSTER'S "OUT-PUT".

Gallery

ENRICH YOUR
CHILD'S LIFE WITH
HAPPY EXPERIENCES

IN THE PARK,
ON THE
PLAYGROUND

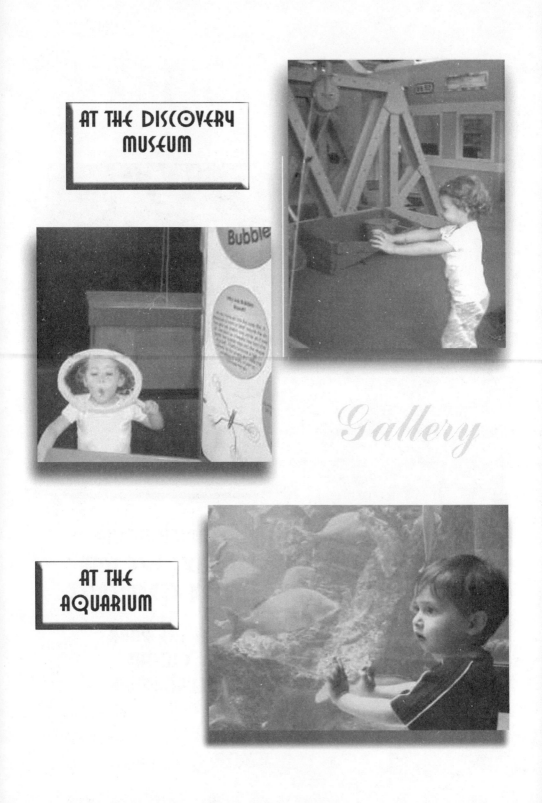

AT THE DISCOVERY MUSEUM

Gallery

AT THE AQUARIUM

IN AMUSEMENT PARKS

IN THE NURSERY CLASSROOM

AT THE GYM

"R" = ROUTINIZE, BUT DON'T ROBOTIZE

Do you still feel overwhelmed with the demands of your new baby, your lack of sleep and the multiple pressures of your daily life as a parent? Don't be upset. You are not alone and your stress will soon decrease. **"PRIORITIZE"** your commitments, include time to **"EXPERIENCE LIFE WITH YOUR CHILD,"** and you will begin to reduce the commotion in your home.

Perhaps you are wondering, "Why do some families seem to function more effortlessly than others?"

The Andersons, for example, always arrive on time with their four lovely, cooperative, well-dressed kids who are smiling and eager to be a part of whatever is happening. Their neighbors, the Greens, on the contrary, are always frazzled, arguing, and late for everything. Their children often look messy and unkempt.

What accounts for these behavioral differences? The Anderson adults balance it all, **what they must do** and **what they wish to do**, because they know and practice the third secret of perfect parenting, reflected in the letter, **"R"** in the word, **"P-E-R-F-E-C-T:"**

Secret # 3

"ROUTINIZE, BUT DON'T ROBOTIZE"
**BE FIRM, CONSISTENT, ESTABLISH ORDER
IN YOUR HOME, BUT ALLOW FOR
OCCASIONAL FLEXIBILITY.**

THE KEY TO ANY SUCCESSFUL VENTURE IS ORGANIZA-TION AND LEADERSHIP. In business, a skilled Chief Executive Officer guides employees and the company as a whole with a directorial structure to insure, in advance, that the firm operates smoothly and efficiently. The word, **"ROUTINIZE,"** suggests that you, like the company boss, establish routines, rules, limits, and a sense of discipline for your family. When you plan and prepare, you can establish order and find time for your needs and wishes in your busy schedule.

You should not, however, turn your home into a total businesslike environment or your family members into automated robots. Allow for flexibility, creativity, and **"DO NOT ROBOTIZE."**

HELPFUL HINT:

A CHILD GROWING UP IN AN EFFICIENTLY RUN HOME ENJOYS PREDICTABLITY, STABILITY, FEELS LESS STRESS, AND STANDS A BETTER CHANCE OF A LIFETIME OF SUCCESSFUL FUNCTIONING AND ACHIEVEMENT.

1. Establishing Order and Organization in Your Home

For an organizational head start, establish your weekly "priority pie" with the tasks you and your family must accomplish and those wishes you hope to attain, from Sunday to Sunday. Each evening, establish a timetable for the following day. Examine the list of activities you have included for your family and yourself. What can you do in advance in help your day run more effectively?

PREPARE EACH EVENING AND SAVE TIME THE NEXT MORNING

▲ **SELECT CLOTHING FOR YOU AND YOUR CHILDREN.** Place the outfits, including shoes and socks on chairs in each bed room. Even a young child can participate in this routine before going to bed and avoid morning delay and conflict.

▲ **FILL BACKPACKS, DIAPER BAGS, PREPARE AND REFRIGERATE LUNCHES AND SNACKS, OR PLACE LUNCH/OR TRANSPORTATION MONEY INTO LABELED ENVELOPES WITH NOTES FOR THE TEACHER OR CAREGIVER.** This works for kids in school or day care and a Nanny who arrives each morning will appreciate messages in writing, too.

▲ **PREPARE YOUR OWN NECESSARY SUPPLIES, CASH, HANDBAG, BRIEFCASE, BOOKS,** etc., if you work outside the house.

▲ **PRE-SET THE COFFEE POT, THE BREAKFAST TABLE, AND THE HIGH CHAIR** with napkins, cups, spoons, bowls, cereal, etc. This timesaver will encourage the entire family to sit together for breakfast and share some conversation about the day ahead.

▲ **BEFORE RETIRING, SET YOUR OWN ALARM TO AWAKEN YOU PRIOR TO THE REST OF THE FAMILY.** This will give you some personal time to shower and dress. You will feel more confident and prepared to care for your baby or to help the older children with their morning schedules.

WHEN YOU ORGANIZE YOUR HOME WITH ROUTINES AND SET LIMITS FOR YOUR CHILD, YOU SET THE TONE FOR:

* **PROMPTNESS AND A SENSE OF RESPONSIBILITY**
* **DISCIPLINE AND RESPECT FOR AUTHORITY**
* **DAILY GOOD GROOMING AND SELF-RESPECT**
* **GOAL-SETTING**

Leslie did not provide a favorable home atmosphere for her three sons. When they came home from school each day, they saw the encrusted dishes piled in the sink since breakfast and the dirty laundry and toys scattered throughout the house. Smelly, fast food restaurant bags were strewn all over the family room where they had eaten dinner the night before and watched TV.

"My Mom and Dad were artists and worked at home. I guess they were my role models," Leslie smiled. "They never cared about being on time or cleaning up and "artsy" people always hung out. We kids were always late for school. Now my boys are late and my house is trashed," she laughed anxiously. "I often have trouble finding their shoes in the morning so they miss the school bus. Sometimes, I get disgusted."

It was not surprising that a teacher called Leslie into school to discuss her oldest son's conduct. "Mike is failing this class. His homework is sloppy, incomplete, and he lacks pride in his work. He's never prepared for testing."

This was a wake-up call for Leslie. With a bit of counseling, she began the process of "ROUTINIZING" and was proud to become a more organized Mom, homemaker, and better role model for her kids than her parents had been. Her previous negligent attitude and excuses were non-productive approaches to parenting.

2. Maintaining Creativity and Orderliness

It is simply a misconception that creative and productive people must be messy and disorganized. You can encourage your child's talents and also teach respect for people, materials, equipment, and scheduling. If you designate a special time of the day for an arts or crafts activity, for example, you are not interfering with your son or daughter's imaginative development. You are, instead, teaching your youngster to accept rules, limits, routines, and discipline. These traits will be beneficial whether your youngster participates in athletics, dramatics, music, or art in the future.

HELPFUL HINT:

INSPIRE CREATIVE EXPRESSION, INVENTIVENESS AND FLEXIBILITY, BUT ENCOURAGE A SENSE OF RESPONSIBILITY, AS WELL. As soon as your toddler seems ready, involve him/her in a variety of innovative activities: Arts and Crafts, Music, Drama, Science, Sports, Cooking, etc. At the same time, teach your child to clean up as he/she works and return materials to proper containers.

Since you are your child's role model, set a good example for cleanliness and order. For example, clear the dishes from the table immediately after eating and wash them or place them in the dishwasher. Clean the table. Encourage your family to help with this routine so you can all enjoy the activity that follows.

Molly was both an amazing, self-taught chef and a tidy homemaker who believed "cleanliness is next to godliness." When she prepared to cook or bake, she first placed all the recipe's ingredients on the counter, to her right. After she used an item, she moved it to her left. When all the elements were in the mixing bowls, on the stove, or in the oven, nothing remained on her right side. Without a word, she placed all the items on her left back into the cupboard or refrigerator and sponged her counter clean. Molly then enjoyed talking to her family while the meal simmered, roasted, or baked.

Life's work is easier when you follow routines and clean up immediately after you complete a task. How can you teach your child habits of efficiency and self-discipline without being a tyrant?

3. Disciplining Without Dictatorship

DISCIPLINE HAS ALWAYS BEEN LINKED TO PUNISHMENT, FEAR AND DICTATORSHIP. ALTHOUGH YOUR CHILD NEEDS SOME DISCIPLINE IN THE FORM OF RULES, ROUTINES, AND LIMITS, HE/SHE DOES NOT NEED ABUSE OR FORCE. If you establish fair patterns of behavior to follow, your youngster will accept and respect your boundaries and understand your expectations.

Set STANDARDS early and maintain them CONSISTENTLY. Acquaint your child with behavior that you and your spouse will accept at home and outside the home. Consider actions that are proper within the framework of our society and within the laws of our land and put those rules into effect.

HELPFUL HINT:

WHEN YOU ENCOURAGE YOUR CHILD'S APPROPRIATE BEHAVIOR, YOU ARE NOT A DICTATOR; YOU ARE A CARING PARENT WHO IS HELPING YOUR YOUNGSTER LIVE SUCCESSFULLY IN OUR WORLD.

BABIES, TODDLERS, AND YOUNG CHILDREN ARE READY FOR DISICIPLINE

○ Before you establish limits, identify your expectations. ("I would like you to sit in your high chair in the restaurant while Mommy and Daddy eat dinner.")

○ Set realistic, age-appropriate rules, routines, and explain them clearly to your child to help her/him know what you expect. ("You may eat, then play with your toys in your chair until Mommy and Daddy are done eating.")

○ Implement your procedures positively and consistently. ("We always sit when we eat breakfast, lunch, and dinner.")

○ Be in tune with your spouse's policies and point of view; you are a team. ("Daddy will not run after you and feed you when you are running around the room and neither will I.")

○ Be firm, but flexible in special instances; holidays, parties, illness, and unforeseen events call for adaptation. ("Aunt Nell doesn't have a high chair in her house, so you may sit on a big chair during our holiday dinner.")

○ Adjust discipline, rules, limits, routines, and expectations as your child grows; maturity calls for more independence and freedom. ("We are so happy that you can sit at the table like a big boy and drink from a straw.")

○ Remember, your child is a person with thoughts, feelings, and deserves your respect, too. ("We will choose a restaurant that brings the food quickly because we know it is very hard for a little girl to sit for a long time.")

DISCIPLINE DURING MEALTIME, BATHTIME, PLAYTIME, AND BEDTIME WILL BRING HARMONY AND ORDER INTO YOUR HOME

TRY A POSITIVE APPROACH TO GET POSITIVE BEHAVIOR:

● **MEALTIME ROUTINES**, from infancy and beyond, should promote healthy, enjoyable, and stress-free eating experiences. Try to eat as a family whenever possible.

■ **CLEANLINESS:** Before feeding your infant, make it a regular practice to change the diaper and wash the baby's hands and face. When your toddler begins to eat on his own, wash before and after the meal; food will land everywhere. As your child grows, toileting and washing before and after meals will become natural.

■ **RELAXATION AND CONVERSATION**: Whether you are bottle-feeding or nursing, always hold your infant close, lovingly. Look at that beautiful face, hum a tune, smile happily and your son or daughter will feel physically and emotionally nurtured. As your child grows and shares a meal in a high chair or booster seat with the family, begin conversation by identifying foods and their colors. Count berries and cereal circles. Read a story or recite a rhyme. In later years, you will all enjoy pleasant communication at the table.

■ **SITTING FOR MEALS:** From early on, set the correct standards with positive dialogue, "It's fun to sit at the table and eat together." Toddlers and young children go through stages of poor eating. Provide small portions, read a story to distract from the meal, or allow time for a little rest. You may decide that your child can leave the table and come back to sit and eat later when he is hungry; however, do not run after your youngster with bits of food. This is inappropriate social behavior.

■ **TABLE MANNERS:** Your son or daughter will learn proper behavior at the table by following your example. If you burp out loud after a meal, guess who will do the same? If you use words like, "Please and Thank you," your little mimic will too. Use positive language; if you want your child to eat with a fork or spoon, ask her to do just that. Don't criticize or yell, "Stop eating with your fingers."

■ **HEALTHY CHOICES:** While most Pediatricians recommend introducing solids (rice cereal, strained fruit and vegetables) at four months, ask your doctor for the go-ahead and for cautions regarding food allergies. Then offer your growing child a healthy assortment of fruit, vegetables, meat, fish, cheese, eggs and enthusiastically encourage new tastes. Let your son/daughter eat what, and how much, he/she likes from the foods you prepare. Always ask for input, "Would you like to eat chicken or pasta for dinner tonight?"

● **BATHTIME ROUTINES and other cleansing activities begin at birth. To determine the best time for your little one's daily bath, first understand your son or daughter's internal clock that tells him/her when its bedtime. When you get "in-sync" with this schedule, you can prepare the tub about one half hour to forty-five minutes before. This consistent time frame will allow for other pre-bedtime, relaxing routines that follow the bath, such as massaging with body lotion, dressing in pajamas, reading a story, playing a lullaby, kissing "good night."**

■ **DIAPER CHANGING:** To reduce the incidence of rash, change diapers often but remember to wash your baby's bottom with warm water, dry the area and apply an appropriate soothing, protective cream before switching to the new, dry diaper. Always sing or talk and distract while cleansing to make the experience less frightening. Your baby may feel cold when you expose her. Be sure to warm the cold wipes, too (dip them in warm water).

■ **BATHING IN AND OUT OF THE TUB:** Wash your baby's face, hands, and bottom gently each morning and as needed during the day. Bathe him each evening, before bedtime; a warm bath is soothing and encourages sleep at any age. Try to have your spouse present to hand you the shampoo, the washcloth, and to enjoy the fun. *Carefully, wash your child's hair with his head held back to avoid soap and water in his eyes.* Lift your infant or toddler from the tub and pass him to your spouse who is holding the towel.

When your baby begins to sit up, place toys, sponges, and buckets into the tub. Blow bubbles and watch your child kick, splash, and play. Babies love the tub when the water is comfortable and the parent or caregiver is calm. Wrap your child in a towel and hug, hug, hug. Clean your child's ears and brush her hair. These cozy, caring routines will stick as your child grows.

THIS TODDLER IS LEARNING TO RECOGNIZE NUMBERS, LETTERS, AND HER NAME, WHILE PLAYING IN THE TUB.

NEVER LEAVE YOUR CHILD ALONE IN THE BATHTUB, EVEN FOR ONE MINUTE!!

Each year, children drown in ONLY a few inches of water.

TODDLERS ENJOY BRUSHING THEIR TEETH TOGETHER, BEFORE BEDTIME.

● **BRUSHING TEETH:** When teeth appear, it's time to establish the brushing routine after eating/drinking, but especially before bedtime. If your son or daughter is squeezing the toothpaste tube or sucking water from the brush instead of brushing properly, do not scream about it.

❖ Try a game with two brushes, one in his hand and one in yours, "Let's count your teeth, one, two, three, four."

❖ Wind up a music box, "Let's try to brush every tooth before the song stops."

❖ Sing a "bye-bye" song to everything your child has eaten during the day ("Bye-bye cereal, bye-bye chicken, bye-bye French fries, bye-bye to juice and milk.")

❖ Set a good example and brush your own teeth while your child is watching you.

● **PLAYTIME/CLEAN-UP ROUTINES:** The value of play has been underestimated. Have fun playing with your child, guiding the process and teaching the skills of socialization, such as sharing. Also, encourage your child to play alone occasionally; this will spark originality, imagination, personal discovery, and independence.

✦ **TOYS AND BOOKS:** When your youngster plays creatively, she is imitating life, developing coordination, learning about the environment, expelling energy and reducing stress. When your child looks at books, she expands language and knowledge of the world.

✦ **CLEAN-UP:** Even a toddler can learn to feel pride in his/her home, respect his/her belongings, and playfully begin to put toys on shelves or in boxes. Sing a familiar "Clean-up" song or create one of your own using a recognizable tune like, *"Mary Had A Little Lamb,"* or *"Do You Know the Muffin Man?"* These words work for either tune, so simply choose one and sing, "Time to put your toys away, toys away, toys away, time to put your toys away for another day."

HELPFUL HINT:

KIDS LOVE TO HELP. BEGIN THE "CLEAN UP" ROUTINE EARLY IN LIFE AND LAY THE FOUNDATION FOR SUPERIOR WORK HABITS.

● **BEDTIME ROUTINES** are often the most difficult to establish. Children want to be with their parents, especially if both Mom and Dad work all day, and feel that they are missing something when they go to bed.

✦ **SIGNALS OF SLEEPINESS AND A CONSISTENT, DISCIPLINED PLAN:** If you notice your little one yawning, rubbing his eyes, putting her head down, seeking a security toy, happily scoop him/her into your arms with kisses and hugs and say, "It's almost time for nite-nite." Don't ask, "Are you tired yet?"

When you pay attention to clues of sleepiness, you will determine your child's usual bedtime hour. Then follow a constant routine, day after day.

Mallory has routinely shown signs of sleepiness at 7:30 pm, so Mom and Dad prepare for the bath together at 6:45 pm. After washing and playing, they clean ears, brush hair, brush teeth, put on pajamas, sit in the rocking chair, read a book, play a lullaby, lights out, relax a bit, kiss, hug, and say, "good night" at 7:30pm.

DO NOT MAKE YOUR CHILD FEEL THAT SLEEP IS A PUNISHMENT.

HELPFUL HINT:

A CALM, POSITIVE, REPETITIVE BEDTIME ROUTINE WORKS ONLY IF YOUR CHILD IS TIRED. GET "IN-SYNC" WITH YOUR YOUNGSTER'S FEELINGS OF SLEEPINESS, SET THE ROUTINE ACCORDINGLY, AND DO NOT BATTLE OVER BEDTIME.

Beckie believed that her toddler should be asleep by 6:30 p.m. because she herself could not deal with the little girl any more. Each night, she put Elana into her crib at 6:15 p.m., but the child wasn't tired and screamed for an hour until she exhausted herself and fell asleep.

Each night after dinner, Elana became progressively more difficult to handle as she realized that her mother was about to put her into the crib. She hid in closets and shrieked angrily when her mother approached. Beckie screamed at Elana until her husband, Jeff, could not cope with the noise.

"This is an unhealthy and abusive situation," he told his wife. "I disagree with that guy who said kids should cry themselves to sleep. Let me try my approach for a few days."

Jeff noticed that his daughter was still playful at 6:00 p.m., so he delayed her bath twenty minutes and then allowed her to play with lots of tub toys. After dressing Elana for bed, Dad read her a story and they listened to some soft music. At 7:15 p.m., the toddler rubbed her eyes and when Jeff placed her into the crib, she sighed and went to sleep without a tear.

If your child does not seem tired, although you are, allow your son or daughter to play while you relax and start the bath routine a little later. When you place your toddler into the crib provide a feeling of security by giving him a small, safe stuffed animal or a tiny blanket square to hold. If he still seems to need you, rub his back, pat his backside or sit on a chair in the room for a while to offer reassurance.

Two days later, place a chair in the hall outside the room and tell your child, "I'm right here. Give your doggie (or Blankie) a hug."

Before long, your child will feel safe and you will be able to leave the room after a kiss and hug.

CAN YOU ACQUIRE LOVE AND RESPECT FROM YOUR YOUNGSTER AND SIMULTANEOUSLY EXERCISE AUTHORITY AND DISCIPLINE?

One does not exclude the other. You are your son's ally when you comfort him when he is unhappy. You are your daughter's friend when you listen to her speak excitedly about something good that has happened. You are a buddy when you calm your child after a fall or cuddle with her when she's afraid of the dark, but you are still the parent and make the rules.

DON'T BE AFRAID TO SET LIMITS AND DISCIPLINARY RULES. Many adoptive parents fear losing their child's love and reward the whims and wishes of their whining kids. Unfortunately, this demanding behavior continues into adulthood.

In blended families, where there are children from each spouse, the new parent often avoids setting controls in hopes of being accepted. This can lead to disaster because a parent needs to be a guiding adult, not a pal.

Carla, thirty-nine, had her first baby after three years of infertility and was thrilled with her new arrival. "My prince can have anything his little heart desires," she exclaimed.

However, Carla's overindulgence will not help her son understand the realities of life. People will not always give him what he wants and teachers will not appreciate a demanding, or disorganized child.

In fact, many undisciplined children are socially inept and encounter frustration in Nursery School or Kindergarten when they must follow rules and realize that there are other children with needs too. Kids who are raised in a permissive atmosphere are often unable to make friends and "get with the program."

4. Setting the Rules for Acceptable Social Behavior

How often do you see little kids running, screaming, misbehaving, and lacking respect for others in restaurants, hotels, or stores while their parents pretend not to notice? These adults have neglected to set boundaries and establish behavior patterns to insure proper socialization.

Although you may wish to emphasize individuality, independence, and respect for your child's feelings, you must still establish limits for your home and the world beyond.

WHEN SETTING RULES FOR THE SOCIAL SCENE:

● USE A FIRM VOICE TO CONVEY A SENSE OF AUTHORITY, "I mean what I say."

● PROMOTE ACCEPTABLE SOCIAL BEHAVIOR, "Let's walk like a big girl. You may not run wild and disturb others."

● CONVEY THE LAWS AND KNOWLEDGE OF RIGHT AND WRONG, "You may eat the apple only after we pay for it."

HELPFUL HINT:

DURING THE FIRST FIVE YEARS OF LIFE, YOUR CHILD WILL INCORPORATE THE SOCIAL MESSAGES YOU CONVEY WITH YOUR WORDS AND BEHAVIOR; YOU ARE A MODEL FOR THOUGHTS, FEELINGS, AND ACTIONS REGARDING MORALITY, LYING, AND STEALING.

Ann believed that her son's teacher should be responsible for instilling values. She didn't bother to correct her youngster, three years old, when he took his older brother's favorite toy. "Forget it! He's just a baby," she told her eldest.

When he removed money from Grandma's purse, she laughed, "He's only eight, but he knows who's got the cash."
The Principal called her in when he was ten. "He's stolen a boy's watch and will be suspended for a month." Ann transferred him to a private school, protesting, "I'm not keeping him home and punishing myself!"

At age seventeen, her teen stole her diamond ring from her jewelry box and pawned it for drugs. When the police arrived, Ann complained, "I spent so much on his schooling and those teachers never taught him anything."

As a parent, you are responsible for demonstrating honesty, encouraging self-control, and patience. When you "routinize," set the rules to help your child function admirably in social situations, but do not forget your child's tolerance level. For example, it is unreasonable for you to ask your toddler to sit still in a shopping cart on a long, checkout line. It is also wrong to pacify your hungry child with a box of cookies before paying for it at the cash register; you are giving mixed signals regarding right and wrong.

HELPFUL HINT:

MAKE IT EASY FOR YOUR CHILD TO DO THE RIGHT THING. IF YOU REMAIN "IN-SYNC" WITH YOUR CHILD'S LEVEL OF PATIENCE AND UNDERSTANDING, YOU CAN PLAN YOUR DAILY ROUTINES AND ACTIVITIES SUCCESSFULLY.

Reasoning with a very young child is difficult indeed, but there are some techniques you can try to help your child cope with temptations in the store. Some suggestions require at-home preparation:

SIMPLE SUPERMARKET STRATEGIES

- **DISTRACT WITH A SMALL TOY OR A TREAT THAT YOU HAVE BROUGHT FROM HOME IN YOUR OWN LABELED CONTAINER.**

- **ADVISE YOUR YOUNGSTER IN ADVANCE, "YOU MAY CHOOSE TWO, SPECIAL THINGS TODAY.** Show me two fingers, one - two. There are many things to see when we go shopping, but we can't bring everything home."

- **AMUSE WITH AN AGE-APPROPRIATE LEARNING GAME.** "Let's find everything that is red as we go up and down the aisles," or "Find all the things that start with B - bagels, butter, box."

- **WRITE A SHOPPING LIST PRIOR TO LEAVING HOME**. "What would you like to buy in the store? Let's put it on our list." This strategy is appropriate for a child of three or older who can learn to think and plan ahead.

- **ESTABLISH RULES FOR PUBLIC PLACES BEFORE LEAVING HOME, TO GUARANTEE SAFETY AS WELL AS SATISFACTORY BEHAVIOR.** "When children go to the supermar ket with their Mommies or Daddies, they must always sit in a shopping cart. It's fun to ride around the store."

When you enter the store, explain again, "I know you are a big boy and will sit while we have a special ride. I will give you some things to hold for me. After we pay for everything in the cart, I will help you stand up and go out."If your child tries to stand up on his own, explain that the wheels will make the cart roll and could make him fall down. "I don't want you to get hurt because I love you. Please wait for me to help you out."

> **BE OBSERVANT WHILE YOU ARE OUT AND ABOUT. YOU HAVE THE EXPERIENCE TO PREDICT WHAT MAY HAPPEN. A SMALL CHILD DOES NOT THINK OF CONSEQUENCES.**

- **DO NOT PLACE YOUR LITTLE ONE INTO A SITUATION THAT IS PREDICTABLY UNREASONABLE.** A youngster's attention span is short. If your shopping will require more than a half hour, select the items you need most and postpone the remaining list for another day.

5. "Routinizing" Without "Robotizing"

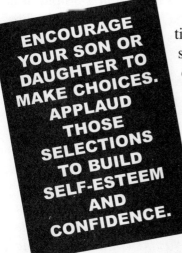

ENCOURAGE YOUR SON OR DAUGHTER TO MAKE CHOICES. APPLAUD THOSE SELECTIONS TO BUILD SELF-ESTEEM AND CONFIDENCE.

When you put rules and routines into operation early on, your little boy or girl will feel secure and confident, receptive to practicing daily habits and learning organizational skills.

To initiate the notion of "planning ahead," place two outfits on the bed or on a chair each evening and ask your daughter, "Which one would you like to wear to Nursery School tomorrow?" Or ask her to select socks to match something you have chosen. Smile and say, "Great choice!"

Her feelings of importance and self-esteem will soar because you care about her opinion and that attitude will carry through to help her do well in school and later on-the-job. Coupled with the practical ability to organize, your youngster will become the "take charge" leader in future social situations.

It is important to remember, however, not to impose a regimented style upon your baby. You do not want to develop neurotic, non-adaptive behavior.

HELPFUL HINT:

DO NOT CONFUSE "ROUTINIZING" WITH RIGIDITY OR ROBOTICS. RULES AND ROUTINES ARE VALUABLE, BUT THE ABILITY TO ADAPT IS INDICATIVE OF EXCELLENT EMOTIONAL HEALTH.

Even after you establish routines that seem to work, always remain "in-sync" with your child's feelings and respond accordingly. For example, if your little girl has fever or a cold, she will not eat a regular meal, want a bath, or go to sleep as usual. First treat her illness, pay attention to her with extra love and care, and forget the usual schedule. Flexibility is acceptable.

On holidays, special occasions, or during unexpected events, it will probably be necessary to modify daily routines. That's O.K. because it is important to feel comfortable accepting change. For example, if Grandma is visiting at 7:00 pm, the usual bath time, but is leaving at 7:30 pm, it is permissible to bathe the baby a little later after she leaves. If Grandma plans to stay until 9:30 pm, however, invite her to join in the usual 7:00 pm bath/bedtime routines and have fun.

Emma was obsessed with enforcing schedules. She told her husband, "My Mother raised me with discipline and that's how I want to rear our kids; dinner at 6:00 and bedtime at 7:30 pm." With this plan in mind, Emma reserved a table at a local restaurant for the immediate family and their out-of-town guests, who were scheduled to arrive in the early evening.

At 5:30 pm, Aunt Lynn called from the airport, "We are so sorry, but we are delayed in holiday traffic and will be a bit late." Emma became unreasonably upset and set a poor example for the children, shouting at her husband, "Your family ruined our night."

Steve, on the other hand, said to the children, "We are so happy that Aunt Lynn and Uncle Sam arrived safely. They traveled so far to see us and we really missed them. Let's call the restaurant to change our reservation and we'll eat a little later. It's a special day. How about a slice of fruit while we wait?" The youngsters felt their Dad's excitement and survived having dinner at the new time.

EXPERIENCING A MEALTIME DELAY?
CURB YOUR CHILD'S HUNGER WITH SEVERAL,
THINLY CUT APPLE SLICES OR A HALF-CUP OF
BERRIES. THIS SMALL AMOUNT OF FRUIT WILL
"DO THE TRICK," WITHOUT SPOILING THE
APPETITE.

HELPFUL HINT:

AS YOU STRIVE TO BE THE "PERFECT" PARENT
WITH A HAPPY, ORGANIZED, "STRESS-FREE" HOME
AND "IDEAL" CHILDREN ASPIRE TO BE "ROUTINIZED,"
NOT "ROBOTIZED;" IT IS HEALTHY TO ENJOY OCCASIONAL
PERMISSIVENESS.

Highlights

"R" = "ROUTINIZE," DO NOT "ROBOTIZE:" BE FIRM AND USE A CONSISTENT, POSITIVE VOICE TO ESTABLISH ORDER IN YOUR HOME, BUT ALLOW FOR FLEXIBILITY AND OCCASIONAL CHANGE.

1. A CHILD FEELS COMFORTABLE AND SECURE WITH RULES, ROUTINES, AND LIMITS FOR:
   - *MEALTIME*
   - *BATHTIME*
   - *PLAYTIME*
   - *BEDTIME*

2. YOU NEED NOT BE A "DICTATOR" TO IMPLEMENT CONSISTENT "DISCIPLINE" EACH DAY.

3. AN ORGANIZED HOME PROVIDES AN ENVIRONMENT IN WHICH TO GROW EMOTIONALLY AND CONFIDENTLY. Give your child opportunities to build self-esteem, by encouraging choices and decision-making.

4. EVEN AN INFANT CAN LEARN RIGHT FROM WRONG AND UNDERSTAND ACCEPTABLE SOCIAL BEHAVIOR; your child will model your words and actions.

5. SUCCESSFUL PEOPLE ARE ORGANIZED, BUT FLEXIBLE; adjust routines and do not turn your son or daughter into a ROBOT.

"F" = FOLLOW THROUGH

Every child thrives on repetition, predictability, and feels secure when playing with the same toy, watching the same TV show or video, reading the same bedtime story over and over again, and listening to the gentle sounds of one familiar lullaby. You can provide your son or daughter with those feelings of certainty and trust when you include the fourth secret in your parenting style, the letter, "F," in the word, **"P-E-R-F-E-C-T."**

> ## Secret # 4
>
> ### "F OLLOW THROUGH"
> **WITH ROUTINES, PROMISES,
> APPROPRIATE LANGUAGE, AND
> CONSISTENCY.**

1."Following Through" with Routines for Order and Emotional Security

Routines will impart a sense of comfort and also serve as time-keepers to help your child anticipate your departure and arrival, particularly if you work.

Wendy returned to work when her son, Micah, was three months old. Like most new Moms, she had been concerned about having enough quality time with him and established a few early morning routines to give her baby lots of attention, love, and nurturing. Before his Nanny arrived each morning, she sang to him while changing his diaper and clothes, cuddled with him in her rocking chair while she held his bottle. Then she spread a blanket on the floor and played with him, exploring one educational toy at a time. When his Nanny arrived, Micah accepted the Caregiver while Wendy showered and dressed.

By the time Micah was six months old, he knew that Mom would give big hugs and kisses when she left for work and again when she returned in the evening for his dinner, some play, a bath and story time. Wendy also gave his Nanny a typed list of activities to keep habitually during the day. Micah would begin with breakfast, a stroller ride to the park, some time on the swings, a bottle, a nap, lunch, listening to music, etc.

Maintaining daily routines not only allowed the little boy to feel self-assured, it also helped Wendy leave for work on time after sharing some loving, quality experiences with her baby.

2."Following Through" with Routines for Good Hygiene

Many patterns of behavior, or habits begun during infancy and early childhood, remain with you throughout life. **YOU ARE RESPONSIBLE FOR ESTABLISHING HEALTH HABITS FROM THE START. "FOLLOW THROUGH" EACH DAY WITH GOOD GROOMING AND CLEANLINESS ROUTINES.**

▲　**HAND WASHING:**
- As soon as your child begins to eat solids and feed himself, use mild soap and water routinely before eating. Carry antiseptic wipes or an instant hand sanitizer when water is unavailable.
- Wash before offering a snack or after leaving the play ground.

▲ **USE APPROPRIATE BRUSHES AND GROOMING AIDS:**
- After the habitual evening bath, look in the mirror together and encourage your toddler to brush his hair. Be sure to say, "Good job. You look so nice."
- Clean his ears gently with a soft cotton swab. It is best not to let a small child try to clean his own ears, so hand him a stuffed animal and a swab and suggest, "Clean your bear's ears and Mommy will clean yours."

- Massage with moisturizer after the bath.
- File or trim nails when they are sharp to the touch and don't forget the toes.
- As soon as your baby has one tooth, buy two baby tooth brushes, one for you to use and one for your child; brush after eating as often as possible, but "follow through" regularly before bedtime. Do not allow your child to fall asleep with milk or juice on her teeth.

HELPFUL HINT:

WHEN YOU CONSISTENTLY "FOLLOW-THROUGH" WITH EVENING ROUTINES, YOU WILL SIGNAL, "BEDTIME," FOR YOUR BABY.
(For example, play in the bath, massage with lotion, dress in pajamas, listen to soft music, read a story, cuddle, kiss, say, "I love you, nite-nite.")

AS YOU REPEAT EACH ACTIVITY EACH NIGHT, YOUR CHILD WILL BEGIN TO FEEL CALM, SAFE, READY FOR "LIGHTS OUT" AND SLEEP.

3."Following Through" on Promises to Build Trust

It is your job to set the example for your son or daughter and convey honesty, loyalty, and dependability. Your child will expect you to be totally truthful, so be sure to make promises only when you know that you can fulfill them.

IF YOU BREAK A PROMISE TO YOUR CHILD, YOU PROVE THAT YOU ARE NOT TO BE BELIEVED OR TRUSTED.

Darlene went gift shopping with her daughter in a crystal boutique and the little girl, four years of age, admired a beautiful $1500 figurine. "Mommy, I want the glass ballerina, please. . . . Mommy, I want. . . . "

"O.K. Stop nagging. If you wait patiently, we'll buy it tomorrow," Darlene replied although she had no intention of returning to that shop to purchase that expensive piece. The little girl trusted her mother and happily danced around the store telling customers and salespersons, "Mommy's gonna buy me that ballerina tomorrow."

Darlene thought her daughter would surely forget about the promise by the next day, but she didn't.

What did this mother accomplish with her lie? She temporarily stopped her daughter's nagging, but she set the child up for disappointment and taught her to be dishonest. The next day the little girl realized that her "Mommy tells stories." She lost trust in her mother and when in the future Darlene asks her to behave for a reward, she probably will not comply.

Darlene might have said, "That ballerina is beautiful and I wish we could buy it, but it is too expensive and we do not have that much money. I saw a little, dancing ballerina on a jewelry box that we can buy if you like it. Please wait patiently just a little longer and we'll go to the store. I'm proud of you when you wait quietly."

Or the mother could have said, "You like nice things. That ballerina is gorgeous and very special. Speaking of special things, let's share a special Mother-daughter lunch today and you may choose the restaurant."

HELPFUL HINT:

"DISTRACT AND SUBSTITUTE" WITH A PROMISE THAT YOU CAN AND WILL KEEP.

Occasionally, a child excuses the parent's fib, turns on himself with self-blame, and develops a poor self-image.

"Mommy wouldn't lie. I guess I am very bad, that's why she doesn't get me what she promises."

This is a potentially harmful pattern of behavior that should not be taken lightly.

4. "Following Through" with Sincerity and Reliability to Implement Discipline

You will gain your child's respect and command discipline when you show that you are decisive and can be trusted. If you act inconsistently or dishonestly, you will confuse your child.

For example, Cody always wondered, "Does my Mommy mean what she says this time?" While his mother was usually strict about bedtime, she became lenient whenever her husband worked late. As a toddler, Cody was confused and cried at bedtime wondering whether his mother would let him cry or take him back out of the crib like she sometimes did. By the time this little boy turned three, he "caught on."

On the nights when Dad was not home, Cody would come up with excuses and delay tactics to manipulate his mother. He had learned that she did not always "follow through" on her word and he could control her.

TO ESTABLISH DISCIPLINE AND COMMAND RESPECT:

▲ **ALWAYS SET STRAIGHTFORWARD AND FIRM STANDARDS**.

When Katie, five years old, called her mother at work, she asked, "Can I bake cookies with Lulu now? I know you don't want us to use the oven when you are at work, but we'll be careful."

Her Mom firmly replied, "I'm so happy you called, Katie. You did the right thing and I'm sure you would try to be very careful, but I will not feel comfortable with you or your sitter reaching into the hot oven."

"Please Mom," the girl persisted.

"I'm sorry, Katie, but I promise we'll bake chocolate chip cookies when I get home. I'll be there in one hour and Daddy will be there too. Then we can all enjoy cookies after dinner. It will be helpful if you get the pan and the ingredients all ready." Katie understood and accepted her parent's promise because she trusted her.

▲ BE CONSISTENT, HONEST, MEAN WHAT YOU SAY, AND YOUR CHILD WILL RESPECT YOU AND FOLLOW YOUR RULES.

"We cannot open the box and play with that little truck until we pay for it. You may hold the box and we will check-out soon," Gail explained to her two-year-old son.

The child knew that his Mom would keep her word and patiently respected her rule and request.

▲ DO NOT LIE TO YOUR YOUNGSTER OR BEHAVE DECEPTIVELY.

Carmen would "sneak out the back door" when baby Luis was busy playing and the babysitter arrived. When he discovered she left without saying, "Good-bye," he was hurt, felt deceived, and became frightened.

Now as a teen, Luis "sneaks out the door" to meet his friends when he is supposed to be in his room studying. When caught, he "tells tales" and has little respect for his parents and their rules. He particularly shows a lack of consideration for his mother.

5. "Following Through" with Reward to Encourage Acceptable Behavior

If your youngster is two years or older, you can discuss his unacceptable conduct and offer a reward if he controls his inappropriate actions:

> *"I was sad to hear that you bit Cameron today. I know you were angry because he wouldn't share a toy, but you may not bite. Biting hurts and does not help you share. I will be proud of you if you remember not to bite in school tomorrow and you may have a special toy when you come home."*

HOW TO USE A REWARD AND ELIMINATE POOR BEHAVIOR:

▲ **SELECT TWO INEXPENSIVE, SMALL TOYS** and ask, "Which one would you like? (The reward is more meaningful if it is something your son or daughter really wants.) I'm going to put it up high in the closet (out of reach, but in view) and you may have this toy tomorrow if you remember not to bite anyone in school." Repeat the reason for the reward.

▲ **ENCOURAGE YOUR CHILD TO USE A SUBSTITUTE BEHAVIOR FOR THE NEGATIVE ONE.** "If you feel angry when someone doesn't want to share a toy with you, ask your teacher to help you. If your teacher is busy and you feel very angry, bite a stuffed animal. That's O.K. because toys cannot feel the hurt."

▲ **REPEAT THE RULES THE NEXT MORNING,** before school and again in front of the teacher who can assist the youngster during the day.

▲ **REWARD YOUR CHILD ONLY IF HE SUCCEEDS.**

▲ **REPEAT THE NEXT DAY WITH A NEW REWARD AND EXTENDED TIME.** "Now you can have a bigger toy if you remember not to bite for three days." Select the toy together and mark the calendar, "One, two, three days."

▲ **PRAISE AND HUG YOUR CHILD** if the biting is under control. If in two days, your child cries, "I want the toy now. I won't bite anymore," and you are on a three-day schedule, stick firmly to your original criteria. Teach your child that you cannot be manipulated. "One more day and it will be yours. Remember, I promised you the toy after three days and you must try for three days."

▲ **EXTEND THE ARRANGEMENT TO FIVE DAYS WITH A NEW REWARD** and hopefully, the negative behavior will disappear.

HELPFUL HINTS:

WHEN DISCIPLINING:
1. TELL YOUR CHILD "WHY THE BEHAVIOR IS UNACCEPTABLE"
2. EXPLAIN "WHAT HE/SHE SHOULD DO INSTEAD"
3. DO NOT TRY TO ELIMINATE THE NEGATIVE ACTS WITH PUNISHMENT
4. PROMISE A REWARD FOR SATISFACTORY ACTIONS
5. "FOLLOW THROUGH" WITH YOUR INCENTIVE IF YOUR CHILD PERFORMS UP TO STANDARDS (If you fail to "follow through," your youngster will never believe your offers again.)

NOTICE THE GOOD THINGS YOUR CHILD IS DOING AND JUMP IN WITH THE BEST REWARDS:
- Praise
- Hugs and Kisses
- Time with Mom and Dad

YOU CAN ENCOURAGE POSITIVE BEHAVIOR, SUCH AS, SHARING, GOOD MANNERS, SCHOOL SUCCESS, ATHLETIC OR CREATIVE ACHIEVEMENT WITH THE PROMISE OF A "REWARD." REMEMBER, YOUR LOVE WOULD BE YOUR CHILD'S "FAVORITE" PRIZE.

6. "Following Through" with Parental Consistency and Appropriate Language

AS YOU SET LIMITS, ACCEPTABLE RULES OF DISCIPLINE, AND "FOLLOW THROUGH" WITH PROMISED REWARDS, DO NOT USE HARSH LANGUAGE, ABUSIVE THREATS, SCREAMS, OR PUNISHMENT. Children who are treated this way become frightened, non-trusting, insecure, and future abusive parents.

CHOOSE WORDS CAREFULLY WHEN YOU SPEAK. "I'll wring your neck," or "I'll kill you," are terrifying expressions that can scare your child and cause him/her to hurt others. Studies show that abusive behavior and language are perpetuated from generation to generation. If you or your spouse had an abusive parent, seek professional help to stop the cycle.

RESERVE YOUR SCREAMS FOR "EMERGENCIES"

IF YOU CONSTANTLY YELL OR THREATEN PUNISHMENT, YOUR CHILD WILL BECOME IMMUNE TO YOUR SCREAMS AND IGNORE YOU WHEN IT REALLY MATTERS. SCREAM IF:

▲ **YOUR CHILD RUNS TOWARDS A BUSY ROAD.** Yell, "Stop!" Run as fast as you can, grab him and say, "You may walk on the sidewalk, but you cannot run into the road. When we cross the street, please hold my hand. Then we will look both ways for cars and trucks before stepping out."

▲ **YOUR TODDLER REACHES TOWARDS AN ELECTRICAL OUTLET OR IS HOLDING A BOTTLE OF HOUSEHOLD CLEANING SOLUTION.** Yell, "Stop!" This is not a toy for children." Immediately, take your daughter away from the danger and say, "Let's play with your toys and have fun."

▲ **YOUR CHILD LIFTS A ROCK AND RAISES HIS HAND IN THE THROWING POSITION.** There's little time for threats or lectures. Move quickly and remove the rock from his hand, saying firmly, "You can throw a ball, but you cannot throw a rock! Someone may get hurt. Remove him from the situation, distract and substitute with another activity.

▲ **YOUR SON OR DAUGHTER RUNS AWAY FROM YOU IN A STORE OR IN THE PARK.** Run quickly and stop your child. "Please hold my hand. I love you and do not want you to get lost. Let's walk together and try to find _____." Later, "I love it when you hold my hand and help me. You are a big girl."

However, it is not necessary to scream when your toddler climbs on the sofa with dirty shoes. Walk over, remove the shoes and explain, "You may sit here, but we don't want the dirt on the bottom of your shoes to spoil our pretty sofa."

Should Bonnie have screamed at her toddler in this situation?

Madison, two years old, left her Mom and Dad in front of the TV and walked down the hall. Her parents assumed she had gone to play in her room, but after ten minutes of quiet, Bonnie wondered where her daughter had gone. When Madison didn't respond to her name, Bonnie ran to see where she was.

"The water's cold!" smiled the child innocently with her hands in the toilet bowl. Bonnie became absolutely hysterical and shrieked, "That's filthy! That's disgusting! Get your hands out of there!" Madison became frightened and began to shake and cry hysterically too.

Although the mother was appalled, she should have taken Madison's hands out of the toilet instantly, washed them with soap and warm water, and calmly explained to the child, "We never put our hands in the toilet because the water is not clean, but we can wash our hands in the sink, in the tub, or in a swimming pool where the water is clean. If you want to wash and you can't reach the sink, ask Mommy or Daddy to pick you up." A simple explanation of "what to do," instead of hysteria, would have been appropriate.

HELPFUL HINT:

IF YOU ONLY REACT TO YOUR CHILD'S NEGATIVE BEHAVIOR, HE/SHE WILL BEHAVE BADLY JUST TO GET YOUR ATTENTION

SINCE IT IS IMPORTANT FOR EVERY COUPLE TO DISCUSS AND AGREE UPON CONSISTENT ROUTINES, DISCIPLINE, AND LANGUAGE USAGE IN THE HOME, HAVE THE TALK NOW. STRATEGIZE WHAT WILL WORK BEST FOR BOTH OF YOU AS YOU RAISE A FAMILY. FOR INSTANCE:

o   Will you both reward for positive behavior?

o   Will each of you make an effort to eat together as a family?

o   Will you and your spouse speak in a firm, quiet tone and refrain from using "curse" words?

o   What terms will you use for identifying body parts and toileting? While accuracy is best, both parents should be comfortable with the vocabulary.

HELPFUL HINTS:

❖   **JOIN WITH YOUR SPOUSE TO SET YOUR FAMILY STANDARDS, ROUTINES, AND LANGUAGE**

❖   **IMPLEMENT YOUR CHOICES CONSISTENTLY - "FOLLOW THROUGH"**

❖   **YOUR SON OR DAUGHTER WILL DEVELOP FAVORABLE CHARACTER TRAITS AND SUCCESSFUL SOCIAL BEHAVIOR AS A RESULT OF YOUR RELIABILITY AND HONESTY**

Highlights

"F" = FOLLOW THROUGHWITH ROUTINES, PROMISES, APPROPRIATE LANGUAGE AND CONSISTENCY.

1. When you "FOLLOW THROUGH," WITH YOUR ESTABLISHED ROUTINES, you encourage order in your lives, feelings of security and dependability.

2. When you "FOLLOW THROUGH" ON PROMISES, you teach honesty and trust.

3. When you "FOLLOW THROUGH" CONSISTENTLY WITH YOUR METHODS OF DISCIPLINE, you provide the guidelines for acceptable behavior:

   - *REWARD AGREEABLE BEHAVIOR; do not punish unacceptable behavior.*

   - *DO NOT USE PHYSICAL OR VERBAL ABUSE; children who are raised with bodily harm or threats become non-trusting, insecure, and abusive adults.*

"E" = ENCOURAGE 5

Every parent wants a child who is totally well-rounded: well-behaved, academically gifted, beautiful, loving, talented, popular, and just "perfect." **ALTHOUGH PERFECTION IS TRULY UNATTAINABLE, YOU CAN HELP YOUR SON OR DAUGHTER DEVELOP ALL THAT IS POTENTIALLY POSSIBLE.**

Begin early in life and try to see your child objectively, accept his/her distinctive personality, delight in the extraordinary qualities, and understand the limitations. **YOU CAN MAKE A DIFFERENCE** by practicing the next secret in the word, **P-E-R-F-E-C-T:**

Secret # 5

"ENCOURAGE"
LEARNING, CREATIVITY, A HEALTHY LIFESTYLE, SELF-CONFIDENCE, FRIENDSHIP, AND SOCIAL ACCOUNTABILITY.

Every baby and toddler will display individual skills, interests, and unique capabilities. Your daughter, for instance, may be fascinated with books and music, while your friend's little girl refuses to sit and listen to a story; she, however, excels in climbing and dancing at the gym. **EVERY CHILD HAS SPECIAL GIFTS.**

Harvard professor, Howard Gardner, proposes a theory of "Multiple Intelligences." Your child can be "intelligent" (gifted) in one or more of eight different ways: linguistically, logical-mathematically, spatially, musically, body-kinesthetically, interpersonally, intrapersonally, naturalistically.

1. Ascertaining Strengths and Weaknesses

Your son or daughter's strengths and limitations may become apparent very early, during infancy, as milestones for sitting, crawling, walking, and babbling are met or missed. Although experts suggest appropriate ages for attaining skills, every individual can develop at his/her own pace. If you are concerned that your child is very far behind in any area, however, schedule a meeting with your physician for a professional opinion.

DETERMINE YOUR YOUNGSTER'S ASSETS AND LESSEN LIMITATIONS

	STRENGTHS	WEAKNESSES	BOOST SKILLS
INTELLECTUAL QUALITIES:	BRIGHT, ALERT, CURIOUS, EAGER TO LOOK, LISTEN, EXPLORE, AND LEARN.	DISINTERESTED IN THE SURROUNDINGS, REFUSES TO SIT, LISTEN, LEARN.	Provide educational and imaginative toys, books, videos, music, art, hands-on activities in short sessions.
CREATIVE QUALITIES:	SHOWS IMAGINATION, DRAMATIC PLAY, ARTISIC S KILLS, MUSICAL INTERESTS, OR TALENTS IN SINGING OR DANCING.	LITTLE ATTENTIVENESS TO COLORS, MUSIC, MOVEMENT; FEW SIGNS OF ORIGINALITY IN PLAY.	Incorporate crayons, paints, clay, music, puppetry, dramatic play, books, videos, and exploratory experiences into daily life.
PHYSICAL QUALITIES:	GROWING IN SIZE, STRENGTH, DEXTERITY, AND DEVELOPING LARGE AND SMALL MUSCLE COORDINATION.	UNABLE TO GRASP OR PICK-UP OBJECTS, OR MEET SITTING, CRAWLING, OR WALKING MILESTONES.	Offer a healthy diet and opportunities to develop physically: reaching, crawling, walking, climbing, dancing, and jumping. (Discuss signs of muscle weakness with physician.)
EMOTIONAL QUALITIES:	USUALLY HAPPY, SMILING, CONFIDENT. AND HAS A PLEASANT PERSONALITY.	TYPICALLY FEARFUL, CLINGY, CRYING, CRANKY, UNPLEASANT PERSONALITY.	Make every effort to extend warmth and dependability to build emotional security, trust. (Even the most adjusted child cries occasionally.)
SOCIAL QUALITIES:	GENERALLY RESPONSIVE TO SMILES, HUGS, KISSES; HAPPY WITH CHILDREN AND ADULTS.	PULLS AWAY, PREFERS TO BE ALONE, DISLIKES OTHER PEOPLE, SHOWS FEW FEELINGS.	Promote loving contact and social interactions. (Discuss concerns about withdrawn behavior with a professional)

Do not lose heart if you discover that your child is not excelling in some areas. Take satisfaction in knowing that you have discovered these abilities and/or disabilities early in life and you have many years ahead to further the positive points and triumph over the limitations.

2. Developing Intelligence, Talent, Creativity

A bright child asks questions and this inquisitiveness represents a direct path towards discovery and learning.

HOW CAN YOU PROVIDE THE PROPER "IN-PUT" TODAY TO PROMPT YOUR CHILD'S SUCCESSFUL "OUT-PUT" TOMORROW?

→ **ENGAGE IN CONVERSATION WITH YOUR SON OR DAUGHTER, BUT DO NOT DO ALL THE TALKING; "LISTEN" ATTENTIVELY**. You will encourage feelings of self-worth and stimulate curiosity.

→ **GIVE THE BEST POSSIBLE ANSWERS AND EXPLANATIONS TO YOUR YOUNGSTER'S QUESTIONS.** Your honest comments will increase knowledge, vocabulary and the ability to think and form opinions.

→ **DEVOTE SOME TIME EACH DAY TO INTERACTIVE, INTELLECTUAL, AND CREATIVE EXPERIENCES.** You will enhance your child's awareness of the world, his/her skills and opportunities for success. Yes, you will have to sacrifice some of your own free time, *but your first priority is your child's physical, mental, and emotional well-being.*

For example, you can enhance language, mathematics, science, music, and art with a visit to the zoo.

TURN AN ORDINARY EVENT INTO AN EXTRAORDINARY LEARNING EXPERIENCE:

Introduce your young child to the animals by name, "That's a lion, or a tiger, or an elephant." Inspire your child further by calling attention to the sizes of the animals, big, bigger, and biggest, the colors and coverings (fur, scales, feathers), the patterns (spots, stripes), and the creature's sounds. Ask your son or daughter to count the elephants, or the monkeys, notice the shape of the ears, the length of the tails. "Who has big ears? Who has pointy ears?" "Who has the longest tail?" "Who has the longest neck?"

Follow the trip with an animal video, a storybook, listen to a musical CD with animal songs, or glue all your animal photos into a collage. Search inside a box of animal crackers for the elephant or the lion, before tasting the treat. Buy a souvenir to remember the experience.

✳ Cultivating Your Child's Inner "Gifts"

Young parents are often amazed, and should be, with the accomplishments of their first baby. They usually conclude that their first-born child is a genius! In our society, high intelligence has always referred to strength in language and logical/mathematical skills. These abilities are evaluated with standardized tests and each child is then assigned an intelligent quotient (IQ). An individual with a score of 130 and above has always been considered, **"GIFTED"**.

Perhaps influenced by the idea of multiple intelligences, The National Association for Gifted Children in Washington, D.C. now describes a gifted person as having, *"an exceptional level of performance in one or more areas of expression."* The organization notes that three million children in the United States are considered gifted.

Other published literature recognizes, but is not limited to, many of the following characteristics in a **"GIFTED CHILD"**:

▽ **Alert, observant, and learns quickly from early infancy.**

▽ **Endless energy and curiosity to explore the environment.**

▽ **Great memory; uses previously learned data in new contexts.**

▽ **Vocabulary grows rapidly when he/she begins to use language.**

▽ **Persistently asks questions, reasons, thinks, and solves problems in unique and creative ways.**

▽ **Develops a multitude of interests.**

▽ **Able to complete puzzles.**

▽ **Collects things.**

▽ **Grasps mathematical concepts: most, least, big, little, age, time.**

▽ **Sleeps less than other kids because he/she is so busy and inquisitive.**

▽ **Exhibits talent in art, or music, or drama, and is generally imaginative.**

▽ **Displays wit and humor.**

ALTHOUGH THE ABILITIES TO LEARN AND CREATE SEEM TO BE INHERITED TRAITS, YOU CAN STIMULATE THE ACQUISITION OF KNOWLEDGE, THE EXPRESSION OF TALENT, AND THE DESIRE TO SUCCEED. Whether your youngster is academically gifted, very bright, average, seems to be a slow learner, or is outstanding in sports, art, or music, it is up to you to provide hugs, kisses, and input that will build confidence and interest in achievement. Your child will enjoy hearing your words of encouragement: **"GREAT JOB!" "GOOD TRY!" "I'M SO PROUD OF YOU." "HURRAY!" "YOU'RE THE BEST!" "I LOVE YOU!"**

Perhaps you have not as yet discovered your son or daughter's giftedness. Occasionally special qualities do not appear in the early years. Albert Einstein, for example, did not speak until he was four years old and many believed that he was a slow learner. His family and teachers did not recognize his mathematical/scientific mind. Thomas Edison became a brilliant inventor, but did not do well in school either. In addition, Walt Disney, creator of Mickey Mouse, Disney World, Disney Land, and much more, was fired from a newspaper job because he lacked good ideas.

BECOME YOUR CHILD'S GREATEST MOTIVATOR AND CHEERLEADER. SUPPORT EVERY EFFORT WITH SMILES AND PRAISE.

TRY TO BE REALISTIC ABOUT YOUR CHILD'S ABILITIES AND BE PROUD OF HIS/HER "REAL GIFTS."

Mothers and fathers, typically, cannot determine their son or daughter's true potential and often set their expectations above the child's likelihood of success. What is the result? The parents are disappointed and the boy or girl is stressed and frustrated.

Eric and Nancy referred to their daughter, three years old, as the 'Amazing, Little Genius.' "Jessica, I know your work will be the best," said her Dad as they drove up to the Nursery School Open House.

The classroom was decorated with charming children's paintings, resembling houses, trees, the sun, but Jessica's paper simply showed four, large paint scribbles and the couple was shocked. "This can't be right," Nancy shrugged her shoulders, but the little girl was excited and shouted, "Mommy, Daddy, I painted that flower. Isn't it pretty?" The couple was disappointed, but the teacher chimed in, "Jessica used her favorite colors, red and yellow. At the beginning of the school year she would not paint at all, but we are so proud of her today because she worked at the easel and made the biggest brush strokes just for you."

Eric and Nancy got the message. While Jessica was 'a big shot' and extremely verbal and imaginative in her own home, she apparently was shy in her first school experience. **The teacher did not give the child false feedback** by pretending to see a non-existent flower, **but instead provided positive motivation by admiring her effort and ability to overcome her hesitation of a new task.** "Great job, Jess," Nancy hugged her daughter and applauded her first painting effort. Eric smiled, "Thanks for making this beautiful picture for us."

"I want an easel and paint at home," replied Jessica. "I want to paint red roses, white daisies, and yellow sunflowers." "She is very bright," remarked the teacher. "You have done a great job introducing her to colors and nature." The couple felt reassured.

PROVIDE THE EXPERIENCES AND THE TOOLS OF LEARNING TO HELP YOUR YOUNGSTER GROW ACADEMICALLY AND CREATIVELY

o **ENCOURAGE READING** by visiting bookstores, libraries, and by bringing books, newspapers and magazines into your home.

● Read to your child at least once a day and discuss the pictures, the story, and the characters; use simple words for your baby and toddler.

● Look at a magazine with your youngster, select a photo and persuade your child to tell you a story about the picture. You will inspire imagination, expand vocabulary and enhance thinking skills.

● Set an example by reading too.

VISIT THE LIBRARY OR THE BOOK STORE AND ASK YOUR CHILD TO SELECT THE BOOK SHE WISHES TO READ.

o **ENCOURAGE AN INTEREST IN SCIENCE AND NATURE,** by planting a garden (in a window container or in your back yard,) by visiting a farm, by feeding the birds in the park, by caring for a pet, or admiring a butterfly. Discuss the clouds, the rain, the sun, the moon and stars. Promote your child's exploration of the world by offering opportunities to use the five senses: look at everything in sight, listen to a variety of sounds, taste new foods, smell a rose, an orange, popping corn, etc., touch a soft kitten, the rough bark of a tree, an ice cube. Talk about everything.

o **ENCOURAGE A VARIETY OF MATHEMATICAL CONCEPTS,** by sorting, sizing, counting, grouping, and noticing the shapes of food during meals.

"What is the shape of these watermelon slices? Yes, we have triangles! Let's count our watermelon triangles. One - two."

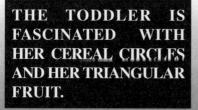

THE TODDLER IS FASCINATED WITH HER CEREAL CIRCLES AND HER TRIANGULAR FRUIT.

o **ENCOURAGE ART BY TALKING ABOUT COLORS ALL AROUND YOU.** "The sky is blue today." "I love red strawberries." "Dad's tie is green." Visit a **Children's Art Museum** to view famous works and **display art** in your home. **Plan time with your child for coloring, painting, and playing with clay.**

o **Bring crayons and a small pad of paper to a restaurant.** Encourage your little one to put pretty colors on the papers and your older child to draw pictures of food: a square sandwich or a round plate with spaghetti and meatballs. **Display each masterpiece** on a bulletin board or the refrigerator to show your girl or boy that you are proud of the work. Exchange the old papers for new projects weekly. Have a "savings plan."

Saving Your Child's Artwork Forever

YOUR CHILD WILL FEEL LOVED WHEN YOU TREASURE HIS/HER CREATIONS, BUT YOU CAN'T KEEP IT ALL:

- Purchase a file box and collect all the special drawings and paintings throughout the year; trim to a similar size when possible.

- Each December, name and date a folder to place in the file box: for example,
  Elizabeth's Artwork - 2004

- Ask your youngster to select five favorites to keep forever; this will maintain a manageable sampling of the work and provide a collection to cherish.

o **ENCOURAGE MUSIC, RHYTHM, MELODY, AND DANCE** by playing assorted musical CDs, classical tunes, jazz, country, popular hits, and children's songs. Your baby will love to hear you sing or hum, and will enjoy the rhythm of rocking and the movement when you hold her and dance. A toddler can take pleasure in a live band or a vocal concert in the park, a children's musical production or a play that is age-appropriate. Happily invite your child to tap on a drum, hit the piano keys, blow a horn, and shake a tambourine or maracas.

When Adam, at seven months old, hit the keys on his tiny, toy piano, his Mom clapped her hands and shouted, "Hurray, Adam. Good piano playing." The baby smiled, hit the keys again and his mother repeated her excitement. Later that day, when Dad said, "Play piano, Adam," the baby knew exactly what to do and waited for the applause. The small baby had not only learned a new word, piano, but also the meaning of encouragement

HELPFUL HINT:

WHEN YOUR CHILD SEEMS TO HAVE A PARTICULAR TALENT, ARRANGE FOR LESSONS, ENCOURAGE FUN IN THE ACTIVITY, CLAP YOUR HANDS, SHOUT, "HURRAY," ENCOURAGE FUTURE PERFORMANCES, BUT DO NOT CREATE ANXIETY ABOUT ACHIEVING "STAR STATUS."

AFTER HITTING THE KEYS ON HIS TOY PIANO, THE TODDLER JOINS HIS FAMILY IN APPLAUSE FOR HIS "CONCERT" PERFORMANCE.

Furthermore, refrain from passing judgment and making comparisons with siblings or friends. **DO NOT BE THE PARENT WHO CONSTANTLY COMPARES HER CHILD TO OTHER KIDS; THIS TAKES THE JOY OUT OF CREATIVE ACTIVITIES AND OFTEN PRODUCES UNNECESSARY STRESS AND HURT.**

Marla, five years old, was excited about "PARENTS' VISITING DAY" at the dancing school and tapped her feet as best she could to gain her Mother's recognition. When the class was over, the little girl ran to her Mom for a hug and some encouraging words, but instead her mother turned to the teacher and said, "That cute, blonde girl is great! Has she been here longer than Marla?"

Marla's eyes filled with tears. She had hoped for her Mother's praise, but experienced a lack of support. "I hate dancing," she lied and refused to return to class.

From that day on the girl avoided all competitive activities, but her Mom was clueless.

❋ **Observation, Synchronization, and Participation**

WHEN YOU WISH TO ENCOURAGE YOUR CHILD'S TALENT, A SPECIAL SKILL, OR PHYSICAL ABILITY, USE THE TOOLS OF, "OBSERVATION, SYNCHRONIZATION, AND PARTICIPATION."

○ **OBSERVATION:** LOOK, LISTEN AND IDENTIFY YOUR CHILD'S ABILITIES AND INTERESTS TO DETERMINE THE QUALITIES YOU WISH TO ENCOURAGE.

Aidan sat near the TV with a pad and a pencil, drawing and drawing. Although only six years old, he made an interesting caricature of the news anchor, a sketch of Grandpa in his big chair, and lots of doodled cartoon faces from memory.

"Look at those great drawings!" smiled Grandma looking over his shoulder. "Thanks," he replied. "I wish I could draw better."

Was there any doubt that the boy would love an enrichment class to enhance his artistic talent?

○ **SYNCHRONIZATION:** PLACE YOUR CHILD IN A SPECIAL ACTIVITY ONLY AFTER YOU HAVE CONSIDERED HIS/HER FEELINGS. TRY TO GET "IN-SYNC" WITH YOUR YOUNGSTER TO DETERMINE WHETHER THE CLASS OR SPORT WILL ENRICH, CHALLENGE, AMUSE, OR PRODUCE FEELINGS OF STRESS.

If your son or daughter seems happy after the session, you have made the right choice. If instead, you hear complaints or see signs of unhappiness or tension before or after the activity, provide an adjustment period of three experiences. **IF YOUR CHILD IS STILL MISERABLE, SHOW RESPECT FOR HIS/HER EMOTIONS AND CHOICES AND CANCEL OUT OF THE PROGRAM.**

○ **PARTICIPATION:** GET INVOLVED WITH YOUR YOUNGSTER'S ENRICHMENT ACTIVITIES.

Visit the class when it is possible, or attend a performance, a team practice, a game, or a competition. Drive a carpool with other children in the program to arouse team spirit and assess their outlook. Assist with costumes or uniforms, serve drinks, snacks, or sell tickets, whatever is appropriate and feasible for your schedule.

HELPFUL HINT:

ALWAYS BE A CARING PARENT AND REMAIN SENSITIVE TO YOUR CHILD'S POINT OF VIEW. PRAISE EVERY "EFFORT" WITH KIND WORDS, EVEN WHEN THE PERFORMANCE IS POOR OR AVERAGE. KNOW YOUR CHILD'S POTENTIAL AND LIMITATIONS. YOUR PRESENCE AND INTEREST CAN SIGNIFICANTLY ENCOURAGE FUTURE ACHIEVEMENT.

ENCOURAGING WORDS:

> *"I am so proud of you for joining the basketball team. You were the best at dribbling that big ball."*
>
> *"You had the best smile in the entire chorus!"*
>
> *"I loved watching you swim today (or dance, paint, skate, sing, play soccer, run the bases, etc.)."*

When the cost of private "enrichment" becomes too expensive, turn to programs in schools, churches, synagogues, or community centers. You may find lower fees, free programs, and skilled professionals offering some of their time.

WHEN DOES A CHILD'S "ENRICHMENT" BECOME "EXCESSIVE?"

Whether you are a working or stay-at-home parent, you want your child to spend the day wisely, learning, having fun, and developing both the mind and the body. It often takes a professional to provide the best training, regardless of the field, and many specialized choices are available for your son or daughter. Whether your selection includes an educational, artistic, or athletic program, remember that it is important to introduce enrichment, not anxiety.

Parents go too far when they enroll their youngster in round-the-clock, planned activities to fill every free moment of the day. The working parent justifies this decision, saying, "Now I know where my daughter is and what she is doing." The parent who is home exclaims, "Now my son is not merely hanging around." Neither adult realizes that their child is over-scheduled, overburdened, and unnecessarily hassled.

Children today, have little free time to relax, play with friends, or try an imaginative activity of their own choosing.

Five year old, Steven, for example, attends pre-school until 3:00 pm, five days a week, and follows with a program of multi-enrichment:

Suzuki Violin Lessons - *Monday;* **Modern Art** - *Tuesday;*
Cooking - *Wednesday;* **Karate** - *Thursday;* **Soccer** - *Friday.*

These activities seem marvelous and geared towards enhancing a variety of skills, but Steven has developed morning headaches and the Pediatrician is unable to find a physical problem. His parents seem unaware of his needs, his feelings, and the pressure this schedule has imposed upon him.

HELPFUL HINTS:

TO DEVELOP A WELL-ROUNDED CHILD, ONE WHO IS CAPABLE INTELLECTUALLY, CREATIVELY, SOCIALLY, AND PHYSICALLY:

❖ EXPOSE YOUR CHILD TO A VARIETY OF ACTIVITIES, SUCH AS READING, ART, MUSIC, DRAMA, DANCE, SCIENCE, COMPUTERS, GYMNASTICS, INDIVIDUAL ATHLETICS, TEAM SPORTS, ETC.

❖ ALWAYS INCLUDE FREE TIME FOR RELAXATION AND IMAGINATION

❖ GET "IN-SYNC" WITH YOUR CHILD'S FEELINGS, AVOID "ROBOTIZING," OVERSCHEDULING, AND PRODUCING ANXIETY

3.Encouraging A Healthy Lifestyle: Good Food, Exercise and Sports

A CHILD WHO IS HEALTH-CONSCIOUS IN THE EARLY YEARS, WILL BE LESS LIKELY TO DRINK, SMOKE, OR USE DRUGS AS A TEEN.

▶ **NUTRITION:**

To pave the road to healthy living and excellent physical development, introduce your young child to a variety of foods, a balance of fresh fruit, vegetables, chicken, fish, meat, dairy products, and carbohydrates. Wash and scrape fruit and vegetables thoroughly to remove toxins, pesticides, and microorganisms not visible to the naked eye.

Avoid an abundance of snacks, fried foods, fat-filled fast foods, sweetened drinks and soda.

FROM INFANCY ONWARD, RESPECT YOUR CHILD'S APPETITE AND TASTES, LIKES AND DISLIKES

Nutritional research on the eating habits of babies and toddlers suggests:

- Kids eat and drink to meet their internal feelings of hunger

- They have taste preferences

- A child who turns away from food should not be forced to eat

When your son or daughter has teeth, offer both cooked and uncooked, soft foods, cut into very small, thin pieces, for him/her to chew, swallow, and digest.

CHILDREN UNDER THE AGE OF FIVE ARE AT RISK FOR: "DEATH BY CHOKING ON FOOD THAT IS ROUND, OR VERY FIRM, AND CAN GET STUCK IN THE AIRWAY."

DO NOT PERMIT YOUR CHILD TO EAT FOOD THAT IS POTENTIALLY HAZARDOUS.

While most parents welcome their infants with breast milk or formula, rich in nutrients, they often neglect healthy nutrition when the baby begins to eat "real" food.

Youngsters between 18 - 36 months, become fascinated with their new freedom to walk, talk, and feel independent. Characteristically, they refuse to sit and eat and reject baby food favorites and lots of adult food. Their bodies still require a diet that includes calcium, iron, zinc, and vitamins.

As a concerned parent, you may wish to speak with your health care provider to inquire about your child's individual needs for vitamins and minerals. Remember, if your friend's son takes a supplement, it does not mean that you should give it to your son.

THE CENTER FOR DISEASE CONTROL (CDC) HAS LISTED THESE FOODS AS CHOKING HAZARDS:

Cheese Cubes
Fish (with bones)
Hard Candy
Hot Dogs
Ice Cubes
Marshmallows
Meat
Nuts
Peanut Butter
Popcorn
Pretzel Nuggets
Raisins
Raw fruit (apples)
Raw vegetables
    (peas, carrots, celery)
Seeds
Whole grapes

HELPFUL HINT:

CONSULT THE PROFESSIONAL WHO IS MOST AWARE OF YOUR CHILD'S INDIVIDUAL MEDICAL HISTORY AND DEVELOPMENT TO DETERMINE WHETHER VITAMIN SUPPLEMENTS ARE NECESSARY.

MOST PHYSICIANS AND NUTRITIONISTS AGREE THAT IT IS BEST TO OBTAIN VITAMINS AND MINERALS NATURALLY FROM COOKED AND UNCOOKED FOODS. INTRODUCE A VARIED DIET RICH IN VEGETABLES, FRUIT, AND WHOLE GRAINS. USE FAT, SUGARS, AND SALT IN MODERATION.

The United States Department of Agriculture's, "Food Guide Pyramid," recommends a wholesome balance and the best sources of nutrients for your child:

¤ **CALCIUM** is necessary for building strong bones and teeth. Include regular milk or soymilk, calcium-fortified orange or apple juice, cheese, yogurt, pudding, ice cream, cheese pizza, macaroni and cheese, and some multi-grain cereals in your child's meal program.

¤ **IRON**, essential for brain development, is found in meat, chicken, eggs, spinach, raisins, fortified oatmeal , and other cereals. (Nutrition facts listed on food packaging refer to "adult" requirements. Ask your physician to help you determine your child's nutritional needs.)

¤ **VITAMIN C** is believed to help reduce colds, infections, and boost the immune system. This vitamin strengthens blood vessels, heals cuts and wounds, and is needed to boost the intake of iron from plant-type foods. "C" is contained in orange juice, grapefruit, broccoli, strawberries, cantaloupe, tomatoes, red bell peppers, spinach, and potatoes.

¤ **VITAMIN D**, produced when the body is exposed to the sun, helps your child absorb calcium that is necessary for building bones and teeth. Milk, cheese, eggs, salmon, and some multigrain cereals are good sources of "D."

¤ **VITAMIN A** shields the body from infections, helps eyesight, and is invaluable for healthy hair, skin, and nails. Carrots, red bell peppers, fortified milk and cereals provide vitamin "A."

¤ **ZINC,** found in meat, cheese, eggs, tuna fish, nuts, and peanut butter is necessary for physical growth. (Speak with you Pediatrician regarding possible food allergies to eggs, fish and nuts before intro ducing these foods.)

¤ **THE B VITAMINS (B1, B2, B6, B12, FOLIC ACID)** help produce red blood cells that carry oxygen throughout the body. These "B" vitamins are needed to energize, so encourage your child to eat whole-wheat grains, enriched breads and cereals, green, leafy vegetables, like spinach and broccoli, tuna fish, beef, and chicken.

❱ MOVEMENT AND EXERCISE:

HELP YOUR CHILD ENJOY AN ACTIVE LIFESTYLE AND AVOID THE CULPRITS THAT CAUSE MANY YOUNG CHILDREN TO BE OBESE AND IN POOR HEALTH:

" **POOR EATING HABITS:** skipping breakfast, excessive snacking, a daily diet that includes an excess of fat, sweets, carbohydrates, and a lack of fruit, vegetables, and grains

" **INSUFFICIENT PHYSICAL ACTIVITY:** little time running, walking, and participating in active sports; too much time in front of the TV and computer

Your infant will begin physical movement, naturally and involuntarily, by waving arms and legs, reaching for a mobile, responding to the noise of a rattle. By three months, your baby may enjoy having her arms and legs raised and lowered gently and before you know it, she will increase physical activity with roll-overs, scooting, crawling, or cruising around your home. By 12-18 months, your child may begin to walk, jump, and climb.

While "walkers," (seats with wheels) do not aid baby's muscle development or walking skills, many push toys do help infants and toddlers gain self-confidence as they parade around the house and the neighborhood, first holding on with two hands, then with one hand, and finally, "letting go" to walk alone.

In no time at all, your toddler will be running, not walking, and you will find it hard to keep up with that amazing, independent pace.

HAVE YOUR VIDEO CAMERA READY: BABY WILL SOON TAKE HIS FIRST STEP."

HELPFUL HINT:

IF YOU ENCOURAGE YOUR INFANT OR TODDLER TO BE ENERGETIC AND ACTIVE, YOU WILL HELP TO DEVELOP A HEALTHY, FIT BODY, READY TO MEET PHYSICAL MILESTONES.
IF YOU RESTRICT YOUR BABY IN A SWING, WALKER, HIGH CHAIR, CAR SEAT, OR STROLLER FOR LONG PERIODS OF TIME, YOU WILL INHIBIT BOTH PHYSICAL AND EMOTIONAL GROWTH.

Gymnastics and dancing programs are springing up all over the country for even the smallest baby and their parents. Some facilities encourage free exploration of gymnastics equipment, while others include professional guidance and a planned program. When you check out your options for your infant, toddler, or young child, always consider these questions:

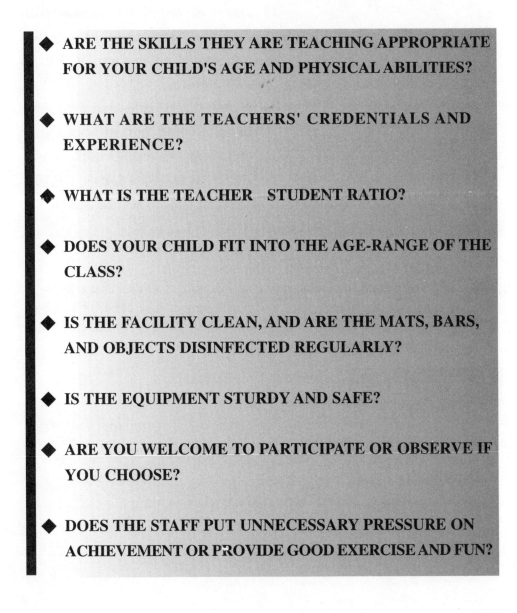

◆ **ARE THE SKILLS THEY ARE TEACHING APPROPRIATE FOR YOUR CHILD'S AGE AND PHYSICAL ABILITIES?**

◆ **WHAT ARE THE TEACHERS' CREDENTIALS AND EXPERIENCE?**

◆ **WHAT IS THE TEACHER STUDENT RATIO?**

◆ **DOES YOUR CHILD FIT INTO THE AGE-RANGE OF THE CLASS?**

◆ **IS THE FACILITY CLEAN, AND ARE THE MATS, BARS, AND OBJECTS DISINFECTED REGULARLY?**

◆ **IS THE EQUIPMENT STURDY AND SAFE?**

◆ **ARE YOU WELCOME TO PARTICIPATE OR OBSERVE IF YOU CHOOSE?**

◆ **DOES THE STAFF PUT UNNECESSARY PRESSURE ON ACHIEVEMENT OR PROVIDE GOOD EXERCISE AND FUN?**

If you think your toddler will enjoy a dance class, select a program in which movement and fun take precedence over formal lessons. Classes that encourage exercise and social interaction with children of similar age are the best and should not last longer than 30 - 45 minutes.

There may be rules and directions to follow and this will help your child learn to respect authority.

WHILE MOVING TO THE MUSIC IN BALLET CLASS, THIS TODDLER IS BECOMING GRACEFUL, POISED, AND SELF-CONFIDENT.

▶ **ATHLETICS:**
When your son or daughter matures, enters school and asks to join a sports' program, encourage participation. The benefits will be physical and social. Find an enjoyable, age-appropriate atmosphere and do no spoil the excitement by becoming overly competitive.

HELPFUL HINTS:

❖ **RESPECT YOUR CHILD'S PHYSICAL ABILITIES AND ATHLETIC CHOICES**

❖ **REMAIN ATTENTIVE TO FEELINGS AND COMMENTS BEFORE AND AFTER THE ACTIVITY**

❖ **DO NOT IMPOSE YOUR OWN INTERESTS OR DEMANDS**

While some kids love rough team sports, like football, others prefer individual competitions like track, tennis, or weightlifting. Perhaps, your child wishes to be totally non-competitive and just wants to dance; then do not force her to try out for the soccer team, even though your friend's daughter wins trophies for the sport.

Bart was intellectually gifted and could compete in academic contests and science fairs, but he was physically underdeveloped, uncoordinated, and hated team sports. Nonetheless, his father, who had played football in high school, could not accept that limitation. He signed the boy up for Little League Football, in spite of Bart's protests. As expected, the boy's inability was evident and the coach suggested he find another game. His father was unsympathetic and scolded Bart for poor teamwork. The boy's self-esteem was dramatically hurt.

Perhaps Bart could have attended a non-competitive gym class to strengthen his muscles, but his father failed to understand his son's shortcomings and feelings. Bart resented his Dad for his insensitivity and poor judgment and when the boy was selected for a national spelling prize, he felt unable to share his joy with his father

4. Encouraging Decision Making, Problem Solving, and Self-Confidence

YOU CAN MOTIVATE YOUR YOUNGSTER TOWARDS SUCCESS BY PROVIDING LOVE, ENCOURAGEMENT, AND RESPECT FOR HIS/HER IDEAS AND OPINIONS. BUILD FEELINGS OF SELF-WORTH AND BELONGING BY INCLUDING YOUR CHILD IN DAILY FAMILY MATTERS, DECISION-MAKING, AND PROBLEM-SOLVING; THESE ARE THE FORERUNNERS OF INDEPENDENT THOUGHT.

Even a two-year-old has unique ideas and specific preferences. Offer choices with boundaries, but respect and encourage your child's view. For example, "Should we eat macaroni or spaghetti tonight?" You are setting the menu limits because the choice is "pasta," but your youngster feels valuable and learns to consider and plan. As he aims for independence, ask other questions that call for decisions, "Would you like to eat in the restaurant that has chicken fingers or the one that has pizza?" The process of "thinking" is set in motion as each decision is made.

Four year old, Kimberly was invited to an outdoor, summer party. Her mom placed two brightly colored shorts and tees on her daughter's bed and asked, "Do you like the hot pink or the yellow flowers?" The little girl folded her arms and stomped her foot, "Those are ugly. I want to wear my blue sweatshirt." Ready to scream, her Mom composed herself and said, " I love your sweatshirt, Kimmy. It keeps you warm on a cold day and it looks great when we play ball, but it is very, very hot and you will not feel comfortable." Encouraging a rational choice, she went on, "Let's open the door and feel the heat. Do you think you'll feel good in a sweatshirt?"

Kim stepped into the July sun and realized that the shirt was inappropriate. She had reached a logical decision with the help of her mother.

HELPFUL HINTS:

❖ **ENCOURAGE LOGICAL THINKING, MATURITY, AND FEELINGS OF IMPORTANCE BY PROVIDING OPPORTUNITIES TO MAKE CHOICES AND SOLVE PROBLEMS**

❖ **ENCOURAGE FEELINGS OF SUCCESS, BELONGING, AND RESPONSIBILITY BY PRESENTING SMALL, ACHIEVABLE TASKS TO COMPLETE**

❖ **PRAISE EVERY EFFORT**

A young child between the age of three and five years often feels conflicted between the desire to grow up and the wish to remain a baby. Nonetheless, this youngster enjoys completing a goal and feeling part of the family.

When Natalie folded the laundry, she encouraged her three-year-old daughter to participate in the household chore, too. "I love when you help me fold the little washcloths. You do a great job!"

Mark praised his four-year-old son, "I'm proud of you when you put all the blocks in the box in your room. You are a great helper and you make it easier for us to have a beautiful house."

The little boy not only felt a sense of accomplishment, but also enjoyed being a vital part of the family.

YOU ARE A BEHAVIORAL MODEL FOR YOUR CHILD:

▶ **WHEN YOU WORK THROUGH A PROBLEM OUT LOUD, YOU SHOW YOUR CHILD HOW TO THINK AND MAKE DECISIONS**

▶ **WHEN YOU STICK WITH A TASK UNTIL COMPLETION, YOU DEMONSTRATE COMMITMENT AND DEDICATION**

▶ **WHEN YOU OPENLY REVEAL CONCERN FOR FAMILY AND FRIENDS, YOU REPRESENT RESPONSIBILITY AND LOYALTY**

5. Encouraging Social Interactions and Accountability

SOCIABLE PARENTS USUALLY HAVE SOCIABLE KIDS. Whether you choose to entertain family, friends, or business associates with an intimate meal or a large party you will encourage your child to share and enjoy the company of others.

At six months or older, your baby will take pleasure in a visit with another family. ***Babies do not truly interact with one another, but once they are sitting, they can play side by side (in parallel) and socialization begins***. Be prepared with toys, music, books, and lots of patience. You might enjoy sharing conversation with another parent, too.

HELPFUL HINT:

WHEN YOU INVITE A CHILD TO YOUR HOME TO PLAY WITH YOUR SON OR DAUGHTER, TRY HAVING SEVERAL "IDENTICAL" TOYS AND SNACKS AVAILABLE (TWO BALLS, TWO TOY CARS, TWO DOLLS, TWO BOXES OF ANIMAL CRACKERS, ETC.); THIS WILL AVOID MANY OF THE USUAL CONFLICTS.

TODDLERS PLAY IN PARALLEL, TOO, BUT SOME SOCIAL INTERPLAY BEGINS AS THEY NOTICE, AND OFTEN IMITATE, EACH OTHER.

ENCOURAGE "DRAMATIC PLAY" AND SHARING WITH:

- **SMALL KITCHENS, UTENSILS, AND DOLLS TO PLAY "HOUSE"**
- **SHOPPING CARTS, GROCERY BOXES, AND CASH REGISTERS TO PLAY "STORE"**
- **TOY TRUCKS, CARS, BUSES, TRAINS, AND BLOCKS TO BUILD "NEIGHBORHOODS"**

YOUR CHILD WILL LEARN TO MAKE FRIENDS WHEN YOU SET THE STAGE FOR HOSPITALITY AND WELCOME OTHERS INTO YOUR HOME. ALWAYS ENCOURAGE RESPECT FOR OTHERS AND THEIR BELONGINGS:

"Let's help Lee clean up all the toys because he was nice and invited us to play in his house today."

RECIPROCAL "PLAY DATES"

PRESENT NEW EXPERIENCES IN A NEW ENVIRON- MENT FOR EVERY INFANT, TODDLER, OR YOUNG CHILD AND PARENT

Sam's mother hurt his feelings. "Last year, Sam, you played in so many homes after school, but this year no one has invited you. Can't you make friends anymore?"

While this mother implied that her son was at fault, in actuality, she had never opened her home to the other children and their mothers resented her lack of reciprocation.

SET THE STANDARDS FOR YOUR CHILD'S SENSE OF ETIQUETTE, REVERENCE FOR OTHER PEOPLE, VALUES, AND RESPECT FOR THE LAW

Your child's actions and interactions with others will model your behavior and the conduct of your spouse.

- **RESPECT THE LAW AND THE RIGHTS OF OTHERS;** your son or daughter will be law abiding and consider the feelings of others.

- **PRACTICE GOOD MANNERS AND USE PLEASING WORDS;** your child will be polite.

- **GIVE CHARITY TO THE NEEDY**; your child will be generous.

- **ATTEND RELIGIOUS SERVICES AND OBEY SACRED TRADITIONS**; your child will believe in God and in religion.

If you close your eyes to your child's anti-social behavior or lack of decorum, he/she will continue to misbehave. If you act or speak offensively, your son or daughter will imitate your inappropriate language.

HELPFUL HINTS:

PREPARE YOUR YOUNGSTER FOR THE SOCIAL SCENE BY SETTING A GOOD EXAMPLE:

❖ **USE GOOD JUDGMENT AND SELECT FRIENDS WITH WHOM YOU ARE COMPATIBLE**

❖ **GREET OTHERS WARMLY**

❖ **EXCHANGE PLEASANT CONVERSATION**

❖ **IF YOU ARE THE HOST/HOSTESS, OFFER A BEVERAGE OR FOOD**

❖ **ACT MATURELY AND PRACTICE SELF-CONROL**

Highlights

"E" = ENCOURAGE LEARNING, CREATIVITY, A HEALTHY LIFESTYLE, SELF-CONFIDENCE, FRIENDSHIP AND SOCIAL ACCOUNTABILITY BY DEDICATING YOUR TIME, UNDERSTANDING, AND PRAISE.

1. **YOU CAN BE YOUR SON OR DAUGHTER'S GREATEST MOTIVATOR AND HELP TO DEVELOP ALL THAT IS POTENTIALLY POSSIBLE: YOUR "INPUT" TODAY = YOUR CHILD'S "OUTPUT" TOMORROW.**

2. **EVERY YOUNGSTER IS UNIQUE AND GIFTED IN ONE OR MORE AREAS OF EXPRESSION:**
   - *Assess and understand your child's abilities and limitations; encourage strengths and conquer weaknesses to develop a successful child.*
   - *Provide varied experiences and the tools of learning.*
   - *Use "Observation, Synchronization, and Participation" to get "in-sync" with your child.*
   - *Avoid stress as a result of overburdening, over scheduling, and stressful competition.*

3. **ENCOURAGE GOOD PHYSICAL AND EMOTIONAL HEALTH:**
   - *Support excellent nutrition, exercise, sports*
   - *Promote decision-making, problem solving, feelings of self-worth and independent thought.*

4. **YOU ARE YOUR CHILD'S ROLE MODEL:**
   - *Encourage standards of etiquette, values, respect for others and the law.*
   - *Practice maturity, good judgment, and self-control.*

"C" = COMMUNICATE

Do you recall those first little swishing movements you felt inside when you were pregnant? Perhaps, at first, you thought it was gas, but soon those non-descript motions turned into tiny kicks and you began to recognize the feeling of life inside you.

How exciting to experience your unborn child's signals and to share those joyous moments with your spouse, parents, and friends! That first contact was thrilling. Then your infant arrived with cries, gurgles, smiles, frowns, new, expressive noises and body language. These communications introduced you to your baby's unique personality and while you tried to understand your newborn, she made an attempt to recognize you. Your infant looked for your face, listened for your laugh, your voice, your footsteps, and recognized your touch.

"*Looking-listening-learning-getting in-sync,*" is important for every parent-child relationship and the letter, "**C,**" in the word, **P-E-R-F-E-C-T,** spotlights:

Secret # 6

"COMMUNICATE"

EXCHANGE EXPRESSIONS, EMOTIONS, AND EXPERIENCES WITH YOUR CHILD

"COMMUNICATING" IS AN ESSENTIAL PARENTING TOOL AND PART OF EVERY PARENTING SECRET

For example:

> **When you "P"- PRIORITIZE, Secret #1, you TUNE-IN AND RESPOND TO YOUR BABY'S NATURAL, COMMU-NICATIVE SIGNALS,** *those distinctive sounds, moods, and movements that help you know what your baby needs and wants.*
>
> *Lori observed that her baby pushed out his lower lip each time he was unhappy and about to scream and cry. This mom learned to 'read' her son's communication and knew, when the lip extended, it was time to change his environment (out of the playpen and up to dance to some music). She pre-empted the tears and avoided an unnecessary emotional scene by getting "in-sync" with his feelings and cues.*

> **As you "E"- EXPERIENCE LIFE WITH YOUR CHILD, Secret #2, you interact (talk, listen, read, sing, kiss, hug, smile, etc.), and BUILD RAPPORT AND LANGUAGE, the essence of communication.**
>
> *Each morning before work, James loved to walk his golden retriever and push little James, Jr. in his stroller. He began this daily routine when the baby was born and loved to talk to his son. "What a beautiful day, James. Look at the blue sky. Not a rain cloud in sight. Daddy has a new client today."*
>
> *The baby listened, his language skills grew, and as the years passed, James and James, Jr. walked the dog, side by side. They exchanged feelings, thoughts, and enjoyed a solid, hon-est, communicative bond , begun at birth.*

"R"- ROUTINIZE, DON'T ROBOTIZE Secret #3, urges you to COMMUNICATE ACCEPTABLE RULES, ROUTINES, DISCIPLINE AND ORDER to your family, to balance your lives and attain success and happiness.

Suzanne was disciplined in her work habits and had progressed to executive status at her busy job. She also strived to be an excellent mother and established routines and rules in her home to keep the family balanced.

When her four-year-old daughter's dance recital and an important office event coincided, she used her organizational skills to plan ahead and schedule her availability for each activity. Her close communicative relationship with her spouse, daughter, and co-workers enabled her to ask for help on that busy day and assure her child that she would attend her performance before she left for her job commitment

"F"- FOLLOW THROUGH Secret #4, proposes that you maintain your routines, keep your promises, and COMMUNICATE THE TRUTH to your child to encourage trust and maintain high standards of behavior.

Bethany took Alex to Day Care each morning at 7:00 a.m. and left him screaming hysterically. "I'll be right back," she shouted over his cries. Although children cannot judge time, this three-year-old toddler knew at 7:00 p.m. that it had been a very, long, unhappy day. Other children had come and gone, but his mother had not come "right back" as she promised.

When she finally arrived, Alex, cried, "Don't bring me here. Ms. Ana is mean. I'm so scared, Mama."

"O.K. We won't come back," Bethany lied and didn't take Alex's feelings into consideration. The very next morning, she dropped her screaming, fearful son with Ms. Ana. Their communicative relationship was of no value and Alex was learning to lie, not to trust or respect his mother.

"E"- ENCOURAGE, Secret #5, emphasizes that you COMMUNICATE WORDS OF PRAISE AND SUPPORT for your child's efforts in academic, athletic, creative, and playful pursuits.

Since Daniel did not walk alone until he was 20 months old, the Pediatrician suggested that he join a toddlers' gymnastics class to strengthen his large muscles and motor skills.

The toddler felt overwhelmed by the other kids who were running, climbing and jumping; Daniel clung to his mother's leg, reluctant to let go.

Lisa slowly introduced her son to each piece of equipment and when the children jumped off the trampoline, she encouraged Daniel to step on.

"What a big boy! I'm proud of you," she smiled. "Hold my hands and jump. You can do it." Lisa's words encouraged the boy to feel more positive.

"Me jump, jump," he said and he let go of Lisa's hands.

COMMUNICATE CONFIDENCE IN YOUR CHILD'S ABILITIES AND INSPIRE SUCCESS.

Each of the first five secrets alludes to the significance of "being in touch" with your growing child through body language, sounds, words, and feelings. The sixth secret, "C"- COMMUNICATE takes this idea into the future:

"OPEN A LINE OF COMMUNICATION" WITH YOUR YOUNG CHILD AND ENJOY HEALTHY CONVERSATIONS, AN EXCHANGE OF IDEAS, RECIPROCAL RESPECT, AND A GREAT RELATIONSHIP IN THE YEARS AHEAD.

1.Interacting from the Start

While the 'give and take' of communication begins to some extent during pregnancy, the actual first cry of arrival, "I'm here! I need you," launches your tangible parent-child relationship. Your natural feelings of delight and protectiveness will surge from within as you gently rock your newborn in your arms, whisper loving words, and provide nourishment.

YOUR BABY IS BOTH A MIRACLE AND A MYSTERY, BUT YOU CAN LEARN ABOUT YOUR TINY ADDITION WHEN YOU PAY ATTENTION TO THE SUBTLE DIFFERENCES OF THE CRIES AND BODY MOVEMENTS. Use these three simple steps:

○ **OBSERVATION:** Look, listen; discover your infant's individuality. "I think that's her cry of hunger."

○ **SYNCHRONIZATION:** Empathize with your child's needs and feelings. "I know she feels so uncomfortable."

○ **PARTICIPATION:** Respond immediately and comfort your youngster. "Here's your nice, warm milk, Honey."

2. Paying Attention to Baby's Sounds, Facial Expressions, and Body Language

Patti was frustrated with her crying infant, now three months old. "I don't know how anyone knows what a baby wants," she whined. She tried to force the bottle back into his mouth, but he turned his head, threw himself from side to side, lifted his knees to his chest, and continued to scream. The young mother felt defeated. "What is going on with this child?" she asked her Mom.

"Listen to those screams. Look at his face all crunched up in pain. He's bending his body as if he's uncomfortable and struggling with gas," Patti's Mom clued her daughter, using her abilities of, ***"OBSERVATION."***

"I feel so bad for him. He is helpless and surely does not want that bottle."   Grandma empathized, felt "in-sync" with the baby, ***"SYCHRONIZATION."***

"I'll put him high up on my shoulder, pat his back and walk with him." Her ***"PARTICIPATION"*** *worked. Within minutes the baby released a loud burp,cuddled into Grandma's shoulder and fell asleep. Patti's Mom had zeroed into her grandson's non-verbal clues of distress.*

ALTHOUGH YOUR BABY CANNOT USE LANGUAGE AS YET, HE/SHE WILL COMMUNICATE VOCALLY AND PHYSICALLY. Listen to the nuances of the cry, look for facial changes, a grimace or a smile, rubbing of the eyes, pulling of the ears, body movements, thrusting arms or legs, an arching back, a hot or cold body, a cough, sneeze or shiver. Don't be upset if you cannot understand your child's special signs. Many parents feel perplexed, but getting "in-sync" takes time and patience.

HELPFUL HINT:

IF YOU FEEL AT A LOSS BECAUSE YOU ARE UNABLE TO "READ" YOUR BABY'S NONVERBAL, 'SECRET LANGUAGE,' REMEMBER, LOVING YOUR CHILD IS ALWAYS THE RIGHT THING TO DO.

WHEN A SONGBIRD IS SEPARATED FROM FAMILY IN THE EARLY YEARS, HE CANNOT LEARN THE SPECIES TUNE. WHEN A HUMAN INFANT LACKS VERBAL EXPERIENCES, HE CANNOT LEARN TO SPEAK, COMMUNICATE, OR FORM RELATIONSHIPS.

Your curious infant will **PAY ATTENTION** to you, too, and recognize you by your touch, motions, and vocalizations. Although, your language will be meaningless at first, your face, voice, and smell will designate food, comfort, and love. As you respond to your baby's instinctive search for nurturing and dependability, you will begin your communicative bond.

How will you transmit language to your infant?

3. Introducing Language

Although every boy and girl differs in the rate of language development, there seems to be agreement amongst current speech experts that there is a common pattern of non-verbal to verbal communication.

THE ABILITY TO COMMUNICATE INCREASES AS KIDS CLIMB "THE LANGUAGE LADDER" FROM INFANCY TO ADOLESCENCE

ADOLESCENTS (12-18 years): Expanded vocabulary, refined writing and speaking skills. Often use words of their "peer group."

SCHOOL-AGE (6-12 years): Speak in full sentences, discuss issues, solve problems, set goals.

PRE-SCHOOLERS (3-5 years): Speak in simple sentences with nouns, pronouns and verbs; talk about activities, feelings, and past events. Enjoy books and make-believe, understand that pictures, letters, and numbers are symbols of things. Recognize their name and signs.

TODDLERS (1-2 years): Use one - two words together; understand a few words. (2-3 years): String two - three words together, use, "no" a great deal, and like to listen to stories and look at books.

INFANTS (birth-1 year): Cry, babble, gurgle, coo, and grunt. Use facial expressions, body movements, listen and respond to your voice.

YOU CAN HELP YOUR BABY LEARN TO TALK:

▍ **TALK ABOUT EVERYTHING YOU DO TOGETHER**: eating, diaper and clothing changes, bath time, bedtime, playtime, etc. ("It's time to take a bath. Let's get your towel. Time to fill your tub with water. Here's your yellow duckie.")

▍ **NAME ALL THE THINGS YOUR CHILD TOUCHES IN THE IMMEDIATE ENVIRONMENT** ("This your crib, bottle, blanket, ball, dog, Grandpa, etc.").

█ **MAKE EYE CONTACT WITH YOUR BABY WHENEVER YOU SPEAK** (he/she will discover meaning from your expressions).

█ **ECHO BABBLING SOUNDS** (When Baby says, "Ba- ba," Repeat, "Ba-ba, bottle." If the baby says, "Lai, lai," repeat and say, "light." Your infant babbles, "Ma-ma-ma." Say, "Ma-ma is here. Ma-ma loves you." Demonstrate the link between sounds and meaningful language.)

█ **LOOK IN THE MIRROR TOGETHER AND NAME PARTS OF THE FACE AND BODY** (eyes, nose, mouth, ears, hair, chin, hands, feet, belly).

BABY WILL LEARN ABOUT HIMSELF AND ALL ABOUT YOU, TOO, AS YOU COMPARE, "BABY'S EARS AND DADDY'S EARS, BABY'S NOSE AND DADDY'S NOSE, BABY'S SMILE AND DADDY'S SMILE."

■ **TALK ABOUT PICTURES IN BOOKS, ON THE WALL, IN FAMILY PHOTOS, AND READ SIMPLE STORIES OR POEMS.** (As early as four - six months, babies can sit on your lap, look at picture books, and listen as you read simple stories or rhymes. Young children love to hear a tale again and again and begin to memorize the words. They are learning the sounds and rhythm of our language, new vocabulary, comprehension, and feel a part of the storytelling process.)

■ **DISCUSS THE VISUAL IMAGES ON TV, ON A VIDEO, OR DVD.** "The girl is dancing. She has a red dress. Her arms are up high. Listen to the drums."

■ **WIND A MUSIC BOX, PLAY A MUSICAL CD OR DVD AND SING ALONG.** Don't worry about getting the words right or carrying a tune. In the eyes of your baby, you are a fabulous vocalist and your voice will magically bring out the smiles. Repeat song refrains ("Old Mac Donald had a farm, E-I-E-I-O") and your baby will learn to sing those words quickly.

■ **HUG, KISS, AND PRAISE EVERY ATTEMPT TO SAY A NEW WORD** (Hurray...Dylan said, "Da-da." What a big boy! If your infant communicates in "BABY TALK," it is vital that you, your spouse, family, and caregivers use proper, clear English.)

■ **DO NOT CRITICIZE OR LAUGH WHEN YOUR CHILD MIS-PRONOUNCES A WORD.** Simply repeat it correctly and your little one will be encouraged to try again.

AS TODDLERS ENHANCE THEIR VOCABULARY, THEY USUALLY GET *'THE LAST WORD'*

Parent: "Let's play with your red ball."
TODDLER: " Ball."

Parent: "It's snack time. Here's a square cracker and a square piece of cheese."
TODDLER: "Cheese."

Parent: "Do you want two, square crackers? Let's count them, one-two."
TODDLER: "Two."

Parent: "Here, son. Two pieces of yellow cheese on two, square crackers."
TODDLER: " Cacker."

Occasionally parents, like Cathy and Joe, wonder why their two-and-a-half year old doesn't speak at all. Cathy sighs, "The doctor says there's nothing physically wrong with baby Joey, but he won't say a word. He's lucky that I always understand what he needs when he grunts or points."

Since Mom meets Joey's every wish without identifying the objects, he hasn't learned the importance of words. Joe doesn't speak to his son either and calls for Cathy to interpret.

Both parents need to use language. When having dinner, for example, "Daddy has green broccoli. They look like little trees. Kermit, the frog, is gr-r-e-en, green, like Daddy's broccoli."

IT IS IMPORTANT FOR PARENTS TO SPEAK DESCRIPTIVELY, PRONOUNCE CLEARLY, AND ENCOURAGE YOUNGSTERS TO REPEAT THE WORDS THEY HEAR. DAILY 'GIVE-AND-TAKE' CONVERSATIONS INCREASE INTELLIGENCE, CREATIVITY, AND RAISE RESPONSIVENESS. SUPPORT FREE EXPRESSION AND ENCOURAGE THE ASKING OF QUESTIONS.

HELPFUL HINT:

DON'T MAKE YOUR CHILD REPEAT A THOUGHT AGAIN AND AGAIN BECAUSE YOU ARE TOO BUSY TO LISTEN OR RESPOND. YOU WILL CREATE A "NAG."

Conversing at home will prepare your young boy or girl to meet new experiences in life with enthusiasm, courage and expertise. A child who speaks well is more self-confident than a non-verbal youngster.

YOUR TODDLER CAN ALSO LEARN THAT LETTERS AND WRITTEN WORDS HAVE MEANING:

Write your child's name (with a permanent marking pen) on all personal belongings.

"This is Brooke's cup," (book, crayon box, toy, toothbrush, hairbrush, chair.)
"B is for Brooke."

Your child may surprise you and recognize her name and some of the letters in new unexpected places.

In homes with non-English speaking housekeepers, Nannies or Grandparents, Mom and Dad need to make an extra effort to foster 'face-to-face' language growth. Young children, like sponges, absorb words from many cultures, but occasionally interchange vocabulary and sentence structures. Listen carefully and repeat correctly those expressions that are misused; you will help your child avoid embarrassment in school, or with friends.

EASE YOUR TODDLER'S CHANGING TABLE WIGGLES:"DISTRACT AND SUBSTITUTE" WITH LANGUAGE EXPERIENCES WHILE PROVIDING BASIC CARE

BASIC CARE	LANGUAGE EXPERIENCE
TIME TO CHANGE A DIAPER AND YOUR CHILD WILL NOT LIE DOWN ON THE TABLE, BED, OR FLOOR.	OFFER YOUR BABY A SMALL FINGER PUPPET AND MAKE A FUNNY VOICE, OR PROVIDE A TINY BOOK TO EXPLORE AND TALK ABOUT IT WHILE YOU REMOVE THE WET DIAPER. Since babies perceive with their eyes, ears, hands, and mouths, be sure it is safe to "taste."
YOUR LITTLE ONE DOES NOT WANT TO GET DRESSED OR UNDRESSED A ND TURNS OVER AND KICKS.	PLACE A SOFT, MESSAGE BOARD ON THE WALL BESIDE THE CHANGING TABLE WITH COLORFUL FAMILY PHOTOS OR MAGAZINE CLIPPINGS. While you undress the baby, divert from the chore at hand by chatting about the pictures, "The doggy says, woof-woof and the cow says, moo." Rotate the pictures every two - three days
YOUR CHILD DOES NOT WANT TO HOLD STILL TO HAVE NAILS CLIPPED, EARS CLEANED, OR HAIR SHAMPOOED IN THE BATH.	RECITE A FAMILIAR NURSERY RHYME, SING A SIMPLE TUNE, OR INVENT AN ORIGINAL SONG USING THE BABY'S NAME. You will soothe your child and redirect attention from the task at hand. "Jack and Jill," "Twinkle, Twinkle Little Star," "If You're Happy and You Know It" are old stand-bys. To the tune of, "Mary Had A little Lamb," sing: "I love (Baby), yes I do, Yes I do, Yes I do, I love (Baby), yes I do, Yes, oh, Yes, I do."

4. Creating a Climate of Affection, Acceptance, and Happiness

WHEN YOUR CHILD IS READY TO EXPRESS HIMSELF, WILL YOUR HOME BE LOVING, UNDERSTANDING, AND OPEN FOR HONEST CONVERSATION? ARE YOU AND YOUR SPOUSE ABLE TO LISTEN WITHOUT IMMEDIATE CRITICISM? If you have established an atmosphere of trust and affection for one another and you are comfortable laughing together, feeling sad together, and discussing meaningful matters, your son or daughter will feel comfortable communicating. **As you** *exchange dialogue from infancy onward, you will feel close to your son or daughter and your relationship will continue to grow strong in the future.*

HELPFUL HINT:

MAKE YOUR ENVIRONMENT WARM, APPROACHABLE, AND ENCOURAGE COMMUNICATION BY SHOWING EACH FAMILY MEMBER THAT YOU CARE ABOUT ALL THEY SAY AND DO.

SET THE SCENE FOR TALKING, LISTENING, AND REAL UNDERSTANDING:

○ **SMILE, SHARE HUMOR AND CHEERFULNESS; YOUR HIGH SPIRITS WILL BE CONTAGIOUS.**

○ **HUG YOUR CHILD AND YOUR SPOUSE WHEN THEY ARRIVE OR LEAVE FOR THE DAY AND SAY SOMETHING NICE,** "Have a great day," or "I missed you today."

○ **OFFER KIND WORDS, A PAT ON THE BACK, OR SQUEEZE A HAND TO SOOTHE AND CONSOLE WHEN SOMEONE SEEMS UNHAPPY.** "I'm sorry you are upset."

○ **SNUGGLE WITH FAMILY MEMBERS ON THE SOFA, IN BED, OR JOIN TOGETHER TO EAT AT THE TABLE AND ENCOURAGE CONVERSATION:** "What did you enjoy today? Did you see your friends? Did someone make you feel sad? Tell us."

○ **LISTEN OPENLY, REFLECTIVELY, AND NOT ALWAYS CRITICALLY.** "I know that must have made you feel so angry."

Even as language develops, you may find that your child's true feelings are more evident in non-verbal communicative signs, attitudes and behavior, rather than in words.

5. Paying Attention to "What is Said" and "What Is Not Said"

Three year old, Chloe, usually awakens in a happy mood. Mom helps her wash and dress and the family enjoys breakfast together. Until recently, Chloe's Nanny arrived just before Mom and Dad left for work. The little girl would kiss her parents good-bye and run to her room to play.

For the past two weeks, however, Chloe has been enrolled in Nursery School and as soon as Mom says, "Let's go to school," she screams, "I'm not going," and runs to her room to hide. Why is this little girl upset? Does she miss her Nanny? Does she have difficulty with change? Is she scared of the new environment? Is the Nursery School experience unpleasant? Does she get along with the teacher? Does she like the kids? Does she miss a nap? Are the activities boring or too challenging?

Although the child has not expressed her problem in words, her behavior is communicating a feeling of distress. Chloe, herself, is probably unaware of the cause of her anxiety. Her parents feel guilty each time they bring her to school although they have chosen the best facility in the area. Perhaps, they need a day with their daughter in the classroom to help them understand the meaning of "what she has said" and "what she has not said."

HELPFUL HINT:

PAY ATTENTION TO YOUR YOUNGSTER'S VERBAL AND NON-VERBAL COMMUNICATIONS:

- ❖ **TO WORDS SPOKEN AND TO THE SILENCES**
- ❖ **TO FACIAL EXPRESSIONS AND BODY MOVEMENTS**

Like many parents, you may have difficulty reading between the lines, but ironically, your small child is carefully observing and listening to you and may already be aware of your thoughts and feelings.

YOUR CHILD IS PAYING ATTENTION TO:

❧ **YOUR WORDS.** Choose and use language carefully when your little one is in audible range. Be open, honest, and always praise. If you can't congratulate your child on an outcome, praise the effort and encourage future efforts.

❧ **YOUR FACIAL EXPRESSIONS AND BODY LANGUAGE.** If you look sad, your son or daughter will too. If you open your arms or fold them, you will indicate acceptance or rejection.

❧ **YOUR SILENCES.** What do they reveal? Your child will wonder, too.

6. Communicating Feelings

Every human being has the potential to experience and express feelings of love, anger, fear, happiness, and sadness. In emotionally healthy homes, family members all understand these emotions and express them freely and appropriately. Children know how their parents feel, how they will respond, what to expect, and what is expected of them; they are "in-sync" with one another and communicate wholeheartedly.

There are families, on the other hand, who are undemonstrative, non-expressive and keep their feelings inside. Their children, as a result, lack passion, compassion, and often feel unloved, rejected, insecure, and unsure of themselves and of others. Parents who are out-of-touch with their own emotions are definitely "out-of-sync" with their kids

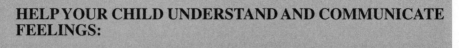

HELP YOUR CHILD UNDERSTAND AND COMMUNICATE FEELINGS:

❖ **TRY TO GET IN TOUCH WITH YOUR OWN EMOTIONS AND EXPRESS THOSE FEELINGS IN WORDS AND ACTIONS; YOU WILL BE A ROLE MODEL**

❖ **ENCOURAGE YOUR YOUNGSTER TO THINK ABOUT AND EXPRESS HIS/HER EMOTIONS**

❖ **RESPOND TO YOUR SON OR DAUGHTER'S ATTEMPTS AT EMOTIONAL SELF-EXPRESSION**

✳ **Love**

Jared was unfortunate in his attempts to express his feelings at home. When he was two-years-old and tried to cuddle with his single, working mother, she pushed him away. "Go play with your toys. I'm tired." The little boy felt rejected but tried again and again to feel some warmth. Finally, Jared gave up.

Now, as an adult he is unable to feel or communicate love to anyone.

HOW CAN YOU HELP YOUR CHILD EXPRESS LOVE THROUGH THE YEARS?

¤ *Begin in infancy,* **set up a caring environment and a pattern of exchanging hugs, kisses, and comforting words.**

¤ **During childhood, continue the give-and-take of loving feelings and fond, verbal expressions; encourage social experiences.**

¤ **Throughout young adulthood, remain affectionate to your son or daughter and support his/her warm, communicative relationships with others.**

❋ Anger

IT IS ALSO IMPORTANT FOR YOUR CHILD TO RECOGNIZE FEELINGS OF ANGER OR FRUSTRATION. SET A GOOD EXAMPLE AND TALK ABOUT YOUR EMOTIONS WHEN YOU FEEL UPSET. IF YOU COPE WITH IRRITATION THROUGH VERBAL, NON-VIOLENT AVENUES OF SELF-EXPRESSION, YOUR CHILD WILL MODEL YOUR MATURE STYLE.

Scott was only two and a half, but witnessed his father's rage and abusive behavior towards his mother after drinking. Mimicking his Dad, the little boy, also behaved violently when he felt angry. He repeatedly threw wooden building blocks at the other toddlers in Nursery School and the Director called Scott's Mother to remove him from school.

"This is not simply a matter of 'The Terrible Twos.' We will not allow Scott to attend class until you arrange for a Psychologist to help him manage his anger and communicate his emotions without violence."

The young Mother realized that it was time to leave her abusive husband for her son's well being and her own. She moved into her parents' home, arranged for Scott's counseling, and advised her spouse that unless he had extensive therapy, she would not remain in that marriage.

Many mothers and fathers first meet with parent-child conflict and a fight for control when their child reaches the active, toddler years. When kids walk, talk, and think, they also wish to be independent. This period of emotional growth is normal and healthy, but often frustrating. "Stepping out into the world" with minimal language skills typically leads to anger, ***"TEMPER TANTRUMS," crying, screaming, kicking, biting, and often throwing oneself onto the floor to handle disappointments.***

IMAGINE VISITING A COUNTRY WHERE YOU CANNOT UNDERSTAND OR SPEAK THE LANGUAGE. YOU ARE STARVING, BUT CANNOT FIND A RESTAURANT. EVERYONE YOU MEET JUST DOESN'T UNDERSTAND YOU. WOULDN'T YOU FEEL LIKE SCREAMING?

HELPFUL HINT:

IF YOU ARE PERCEPTIVE, IN-SYNC WITH YOUR CHILD, YOU CAN OCCASIONALLY PLAN AHEAD AND AVOID A TANTRUM.

Maryanne, for example, knows that every time they go to the supermarket, little Jorge wants a balloon. When Maryanne places the string into the boy's hand, he holds on tightly, looks up at his "treasure," and sits in the cart with a big smile on his face. Shopping is easy. When Maryanne refuses to buy a balloon, Jorge screams or tries to climb out of the cart. The little boy is upset, and cannot understand his mother's inconsistency.

The solution is simple and certainly not worth fighting about. Children appreciate regularity and feel secure with repetition; therefore, if Maryanne takes Jorge to the same supermarket where she has bought balloons upon occasion, she needs to anticipate and avoid the problem by purchasing the balloon when they enter the store. If she prefers not to give her son the inflatable toy, she should shop in a totally different market where balloons are not flaunted overhead.

IF YOU ARGUE OVER ISSUES THAT ARE NOT OF MAJOR IMPORTANCE, YOU, NOT YOUR TODDLER, WILL BE THE ONE INITIATING AN UNNECESSARY POWER STRUGGLE

Since your son or daughter will face many new challenges each day, *avoid situations that you know will cause a tantrum.* Choose your battles wisely, exerting authority only when your child's actions will put him/her, or others, in physical danger. For example:

Charlie Ann wants to put her finger in the socket even though you have told her, "No! That's hot." Stand firm. A safety issue calls for confrontation. Pick up your daughter and try to "distract" from the socket "and substitute" something safe to handle. If diversion doesn't work and your little one throws herself on the floor, screams and kicks, leave her there if the space is safe or lift and relocate her to a safer place until the anger passes. Do not try to reason with your child during the tantrum, because she will not hear you.

When everyone is calm, explain, "I love you and don't want you to get hurt. I feel bad when you are unhappy. Please talk to me when you feel angry. Tell me why you are upset. I can't help you when you scream."

✳ Fear

LIKE EVERY INDIVIDUAL, YOUR CHILD WILL HAVE SOME FEARS AND IT IS YOUR JOB TO HELP YOUR YOUNGSTER COMMUNICATE AND OVERCOME THOSE ANXIOUS FEELINGS. Fear of the dark is common. Reassure with a nightlight and a favorite soft toy. Play quiet music at bedtime to eliminate feelings of being alone. An extra kiss and hug helps nighttime uncertainties disappear, as well. Ask questions when your child cries at night. "What makes you feel that way?" Be sure to listen and offer simple words of comfort.

SHOW YOUR SUPPORT, LOVE, AND NEVER LAUGH WHEN YOUR CHILD FEELS FRIGHTENED. THE ANXIETY IS REAL AND YOUR YOUNGSTER WILL NO LONGER TRUST YOU OR CONFIDE IN YOU IF YOU DISREGARD HIS/HER FEELINGS.

HELPFUL HINT:

TELL A "PARALLEL STORY" TO HELP YOUR CHILD COPE WITH A PROBLEM, FEAR, OR CONCERN.

"Uncle Joey was scared of the dark when he was a little boy, just like you. His Mommy put a flashlight under his pillow and whenever he felt afraid, he turned it on, looked around his dark room, and couldn't find anything scary. Then he went to sleep feeling very happy and safe.

Here's a flashlight for you, just like Uncle Joey's. Let's try to turn it on and look all around the room. Do you see anything scary?"

✳ Happiness and Sadness

IF YOU HAVE OPTIMISTIC, HAPPY SURROUNDINGS IN YOUR HOME, YOUR CHILD WILL THRIVE, LEARN TO SMILE, LAUGH, AND COMMUNICATE JOY TO OTHERS. Your youngster will mirror your facial expressions, body language and attitude. If your baby looks sad, perhaps that is the feeling that you are conveying.

Three-year-old, Taylor, seemed to love her morning nursery school class and participated in the arts and crafts corner, then went to the puzzle table, and continued from activity to activity, smiling, laughing, and talking to her classmates and teachers. She enjoyed music and story time too, but when the teacher announced, "Time to go home," Taylor's face turned solemn.

"Is everything O.K?" asked Miss Kim as she walked the children to the dismissal area. "This is the sad face my mommy has when she sees me," the little girl replied grimly.

When the car approached the school with Taylor's mom at the wheel, the teacher understood. Instead of greeting her daughter with enthusiasm, the mother sat speechless and looked miserable while the teacher buckled her child into the car. How depressing for a little girl to experience the rejecting stares of her mother! Was this woman so unhappy to see her youngster or did she have other problems?

It is important to be honest with yourself, your spouse, and your child. If there is a reason for sadness, such as illness, or a loss, express those feelings so your child does not misinterpret your emotions as personal rejection.

YOUR CHILD NEEDS TO KNOW THAT IT IS NORMAL TO FEEL UNHAPPY WHEN SOMETHING BAD HAS HAPPENED

If you feel unhappy everyday, however, that is not natural and you need to obtain professional help to ascertain your problem. Do not allow your sorrow to overtake your life and hurt your spouse and your child. Make every effort to lift your spirits when your child is with you and say, "I love you," even when you feel down. Occasionally a child mistakenly feels responsible for a parent's melancholy and suffers as well.

7. Tuning-in to Behavioral Changes

It may surprise you that your infant or toddler has strong feelings and opinions, likes and dislikes, moods and attitudes, but everything can change, even daily, as your child grows.

HELPFUL HINT:

WHEN YOU NOTICE A CHANGE IN YOUR YOUNGSTER'S BEHAVIOR OR EMOTIONAL REACTIONS, IT IS A "COMMUNICATIVE SIGNAL" THAT YOU NEED TO CHANGE, TOO.

For example, during his fifth and sixth months, Ben spent day after day playing in a "saucer-like toy," designed to entertain a baby. He enjoyed grabbing and tasting the many little objects on the toy's perimeter and his Mom enjoyed the free time and convenience.

When Ben reached his seventh month, however, he began to cry whenever his mother tried to place him into the seat. "I don't know why he cries. He used to love it," she complained to her friend.

"Kids change. My baby has refused to go into that seat for the last two months," her friend retorted. "She's past the stage of simply touching and tasting. Now she loves to crawl throughout the house and pull up on the furniture. That toy restricted her movement."

Ben's mother suddenly realized that her baby was communicating his needs. At seven months of age, babies need to strengthen their arms and legs. They need to move about the home to explore the envionment as a prelude to walking.

Ben was actually his own developmental advocate and his mother was unknowingly hurting his progress.

YOUR CHILD'S SMILES OR TEARS AND BODY LANGUAGE WILL REVEAL THE APPROPRIATENESS OF A TOY. A HAPPY CHILD = AN IDEAL PLAYTHING.

Even as your child matures and speaks fluently, he/she may choose to keep quiet about his/her real thoughts and feelings. Only a skillful parent who is "in-sync" with a youngster can 'read the signal' of a behavioral change or a problem.

Occasionally, a child who is in touch with his parents' feelings will concoct a story to make his Mom or Dad happy. For example:

Joanna did not always listen to her children when they spoke, but her kids were sharp and noticed the comments that captured her response. As they matured, they began telling her what she wanted to hear.

When Joanna's first grader, Zack, failed a test, he contrived a story for his Mother. "My teacher's not fair!" Joanna looked up. "I studied my spelling words for hours, but she tested us on words we never saw." Joanna believed the boy and blamed the teacher for her son's failure, "They should fire that woman!"

*Zack, only six years old, had already learned to **"HIDE THE TRUTH BY TELLING HIS MOTHER WHAT SHE PREFERED, TO ASSIGN BLAME TO ANOTHER INDIVIDUAL FOR HIS DEFICIENCIES."***

Dishonesty in early communicative interactions will hurt future parent-child exchanges. When Zack becomes a teen, he will narrate other imaginary tales to match his parent's selective hearing.

HELPFUL HINTS:

❖ **TO ENJOY AN OPEN, SINCERE RELATIONSHIP WITH YOUR SON OR DAUGHTER, LISTEN OPENLY, NOT SELECTIVELY. DO NOT EVOKE WHAT YOU PREFER TO HEAR.**

❖ **IF YOU WANT YOUR CHILD TO CONFIDE IN YOU IN THE FUTURE, ACCEPT ALL OF TODAY'S COMMUNICATIONS WITHOUT JUDGMENT OR CRITICISM.**

8. Establishing Contact for a Lifetime

If you pay attention to your young child, you will not only raise a brighter, more sociable youngster, you will also begin a relationship of communication that will last throughout the growing years and into the future.

Secret #6, "Communicate," emphasizes the importance of interacting with your baby from the very beginning, learning to understand non-verbal clues, helping your child to acquire language, and establishing an honest relationship that will continue to grow throughout the years. "Perfect" Parenting implies that you:

OPEN A PERMANENT PARENT-CHILD COMMUNICATIONS' CHANNEL:

- **ENCOURAGE YOUR CHILD TO SPEAK WITH YOU, FROM INFANCY ONWARD, AND ALWAYS PROMOTE THE TRUTH.**

- **WHEN YOUR CHILD TALKS, PAY ATTENTION TO EVERY WORD AND LAY THE FOUNDATION FOR A LOVING, AMICABLE RELATIONSHIP.** When you listen, your child realizes that you care. If you ignore your baby when he is babbling and trying to make contact, he will feel alone and isolated.

- **OBSERVE THE EMOTION ATTACHED TO YOUR CHILD'S WORDS.** This will give you insight into your youngster's feelings.

- **CREATE A SUPPORTIVE, HAPPY HOME ENVIRONMENT IN WHICH EVERYONE FEELS COMFORTABLE EXCHANGING IDEAS, DREAMS, AND OPINIONS.** If you create a cold climate in your home, you will shut your child out today and in the future.

Highlights

"C" = "COMMUNICATE" WITH YOUR CHILD FROM THE START; EXCHANGE EXPRESSIONS, EMOTIONS, AND EXPERIENCES TO OPEN A LINE OF COMMUNICATION FOR THE FUTURE.

1. Communication begins with "Paying Attention" through:
   - *OBSERVATION: Look, listen and discover sounds, facial expressions, and body language.*
   - *SYNCHRONIZATION: Empathize with your child's needs, feelings, and interests.*
   - *PARTICIPATION: Respond immediately to "what is said" and "what is not said" and comfort your child.*

2. Loving and soothing your child is always the right thing to do when you cannot understand his/her non-verbal communications.

3. MAKE EVERY SHARED MOMENT A LANGUAGE ENCOUNTER; if you talk to your baby, he will learn to talk to you.

4. "Distract and substitute" with language experiences while providing basic care.

5. Create a climate of love and acceptance to encourage truthful communications:
   - *Do not encourage your child to tell you only what you want to hear.*
   - *Do not make excuses or pass the blame for problems or poor behavior.*

6. Help your child learn to express his/her feelings and establish an open channel of communication for a lifetime.

When you engage your child in a variety of activities, you offer multiple opportunities for the development of communication skills

This toddler (left) is communicating his sense of humor as he removes one peg and replaces it with half of his "banana." How imaginative!

This little girl (right) is developing physical, social, and communication skills as she follows the teacher's verbal directions at ballet and interacts with her friends.

These toddlers are learning to socialize, co-operate, and communicate

"T" = TEACH, TEACH, TEACH

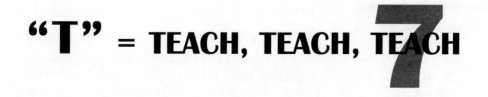

Who is your child's first and most influential teacher? You are, of course.

REGARDLESS OF YOUR EDUCATIONAL BACKGROUND OR DESIRE TO INSTRUCT, YOU AND YOUR SPOUSE ARE RESPONSIBLE FOR THE DIFFICULT TASK OF HELPING YOUR CHILD TO GROW AS A PERSON, TO REACH POTENTIAL, AND TO FUNCTION SUCCESSFULLY IN OUR SOCIETY.

The letter "T," last in the word **P-E-R-F-E-C-T,** is certainly not least in importance; the seventh secret reminds you to use your wisdom and your experience to "Teach" your child from infancy to adulthood. Surely there will be many professionals to provide information and offer training to your son or daughter during the coming years, but from the start, **YOU WILL UNKNOWINGLY CONVEY ACADEMIC AND PHYSICAL SKILLS, MORALS, ETHICS, VALUES, HABITS, AND SOCIAL BEHAVIOR. CLEARLY, YOU ARE YOUR CHILD'S ROLE MODEL.**

Secret # 7

"TEACH, TEACH, TEACH"

SELF-AWARENESS AND KNOWLEDGE OF THE WORLD

HELPFUL HINT:

EVERY CHILD LOVES TO MIMIC A PARENT'S FACIAL EXPRESSIONS, BODY MOVEMENTS, LANGUAGE, EMOTIONS, AND BEHAVIOR. MAKE EVERY EFFORT TO SET A GOOD EXAMPLE WITH ALL YOU SAY AND DO.

Do not use words or thoughts you do not wish to have repeated because your child will surely express everything without holding back:

Stacy disliked her mother-in-law. "That woman is a pain in my you-know-what," she told her friend on the phone while her daughter played in the adjoining room. "She thinks she's the Queen and my husband puts her up on a throne."

Later that day, the in-laws arrived and four year-old, Brittany, ran to greet them at the door. "Come Grandma," she took the lady's hand. "Sit on this big chair like a Queen. Maybe you won't give Mommy that pain in her you-know-what anymore."

Stacy was mortified! She did not realize that her daughter had listened to her. Although the words were slightly misconstrued, the gist of her conversation led to an extremely embarrassing moment.

By communicating with your child daily, questioning and listening with great interest, you will supplement your son or daughter's education.

"What was the most fun in school today?" "Did you paint or color with crayons? What songs did you sing? Please sing one for me." "What did you share in school with your friends?" "What made you feel sad today?"

THROUGH EXPERIENCES AND COMMUNICATIONS WITH YOUR CHILD, YOU WILL STIMULATE INTELLECTUAL, ATHLETIC, CREATIVE, EMOTIONAL, AND SOCIAL DEVELOPMENT. YOUR YOUNGSTER WILL APPRECIATE YOUR INTEREST AND IN TURN BECOME MORE ENTHUSED ABOUT LEARNING.

1. Teaching Intellectual Skills

HELPFUL HINT:

CHILDREN LEARN BEST IN A STRESS-FREE, PLAYFUL SETTING. CREATE FUN OPPORTUNITIES AND YOUR CHILD WILL LEARN.

Jill had always been extremely bright in school and wanted her baby girl, Sydney, to have an academic head start. When her daughter reached ten months old, the ambitious Mom wished to teach her the alphabet and purchased, "Flash cards for First Graders." The baby was not interested in meaningless, squiggly lines on those cards and the complicated accompanying pictures. Jill became frustrated.

Her husband, however, stacked the colorful alphabet blocks up high for his daughter and named the letters and the simple pictures on the blocks. She became familiar with them as they knocked down the block pile and Daddy laughed, "The "B" fell down." Sydney laughed too as Dad built the alphabet tower again.

When Grandma came to visit each week, she sang to Sydney from the colorful pages of a children's musical book. The baby clapped her hands and when Grandma sang, "A, B, C," little Sydney yelled, "D," to everyone's surprise.

✱ **Developing A Love for Language: Talking, Reading, and Writing**

When you expose your child to a variety of language experiences, through talking, reading, and writing, you increase a love for communication and the desire to be in contact with others. Children with good language skills excel academically and socially. Moreover, an individual who expresses himself well feels self-confident and usually succeeds in life.

(By using the simple strategies in the previous chapter, pages 148-150, **"You Can Help Your Baby Learn to Talk,"** you can build language skills in the very early years.)

ACQUAINT YOUR GROWING CHILD WITH SPOKEN AND WRITTEN LANGUAGE THROUGHOUT THE DAY

- ■ **WHETHER YOU HAVE A TODDLER OR OLDER CHILD, USE A VARIETY OF EXPRESSIONS IN GRAMMATICALLY CORRECT SENTENCES WHENEVER YOU INTERACT.** You will demonstrate the structure and rules of our language.

- ■ **TURN BREAKFAST, LUNCH, AND DINNER CONVERSATIONS INTO DAILY LANGUAGE-LEARNING OPPORTUNITIES:** "You have green peas and orange carrots for lunch with your chicken. They are Grandpa's favorite vegetables. Mommy has a different lunch, but I have the color green too. Do you see something green on my plate? Good! I have green lettuce and spinach in my salad." You have introduced the concept of same and different, stimulated the eyes and the mind to compare and contrast and helped your child listen, think, and speak.

- ■ **ENCOURAGE YOUR CHILD TO TALK ON THE TELEPHONE TO "PATIENT" FAMILY MEMBERS OR FRIENDS.** Even if your little one only listens, she will become accustomed to the sounds of conversation.

- ■ **TELL A SIMPLE STORY USING FAMILIAR NAMES OF PEOPLE, PETS, OR FAMILIAR OBJECTS IN THE HOME AND ASK YOUR CHILD TO RETELL THE TALE.** Hearing the names of recognizable things will be fun, but listening and repeating the story will stimulate comprehension and memory. If you have a toddler, you can retell the story together by asking your son or daughter to fill in a word that he/she can say easily. For example, "This is a story about Rover. Rover is a _____."

■ **EXPAND VOCABULARY BY USING AND EXPLAINING NEW WORDS OFTEN. NEW EXPRESSIONS WILL COME ALIVE IN THE KITCHEN AS YOU "COOK" TOGETHER.** Discuss the ingredients of a meal, your cooking responsibilities, and the tools you use in food preparation. For example, "I'll chop the red tomatoes and the yellow peppers and you can put them into our green, chopped salad." Even a toddler can talk about mixing pudding, mashing potatoes, or spreading cream cheese on bread with a safe utensil. Children also love to shake sprinkles on cookies or on a big ice cream sundae and talk about the process.

■ **DO NOT LIMIT READING TO A PRE-BEDTIME ROUTINE. BRING A BOOK TO READ WHILE WAITING IN A RESTAURANT, WHILE ENJOYING A SNACK AT HOME, WHILE SITTING ON A BENCH IN THE PARK, ON AN AIRPLANE, AT THE BEACH, OR ON THE WAY TO GRANDMA'S HOUSE.**

■ **POINT OUT COLORS, LETTERS, AND NUMBERS IN YOUR SURROUNDINGS, ON SIGNS, ON CEREAL BOXES, IN STORES, ON RESTAURANT MENUS.** "The sun is yellow." "Your hat is blue and Mommy's sweater is blue." "What color is the stop sign? See the S-T-O-P?" As your child matures, introduce the "written color words" on crayons and show your child letters that can have meaning, such as, "K is for Kix cereal, and for you - KIRSTEN!"

■ **PROVIDE YOUR TODDLER WITH A DECK OF SIMPLE "PICTURE," CARDS AND YOUR PRE-SCHOOLER WITH "LETTER" OR "NUMBER" CARDS.** Identify the pictures, letters, or numbers while riding in a car or waiting on a line. Your child will soon recite them back to you.

- **LISTEN TO SONGS, POEMS, OR TALES ON CDs OR VIDEOS TO OBTAIN LANGUAGE IN NEW EXCITING WAYS.** It is best to join in the listening and viewing experiences to make comments and explain what you both see and hear. Do not use technical, educational tools, such as TVs, Videos, DVDs, and computers as daily babysitters.

- **SING A TUNE OR RECITE A POEM AND EMPHASIZE THE RHYMING WORDS BY SAYING THEM SLIGHTLY LOUDER.** "Jack and JILL, Went up the HILL." **TAP YOUR KNEE AS YOUR RECITE THE WORDS AND ACCENTUATE THE RHYTHM.**

- **CREATE YOUR CHILD'S NAME IN LARGE, TEXTURED LETTERS. FORM EACH ONE WITH WHITE GLUE, SPRINKLED WITH DRY OATMEAL OR CEREAL CIRCLES. WHEN IT IS DRY, ENCOURAGE YOUR CHILD TO FEEL THE LETTER FORMATIONS OF HIS/HER NAME.** This pre-writing skill can be introduced at 2 ½ - 3 years of age.

- **PLAY LETTER AND WORD GAMES ON THE COMPUTER** and if your child expresses an interest, verbally **CONNECT LETTERS AND SOUNDS TO WORDS:** "B" is for b-b-bus, b-b--book, b-baby, bottle, "F" is for f-f-fan, f-f-fish, f-foot, f-food.

HELPFUL HINTS:

- ❖ **WHEN YOUR BABY TRIES TO "SPEAK" TO YOU WITH TINY VOCALIZATIONS, RESPOND WITH LOVE, EXCITEMENT, AND CONFIRMATION.**

- ❖ **PAY CLOSE ATTENTION TO THOSE SOUNDS AND VALUE EVERY UTTERANCE. YOU WILL ENCOURAGE MORE VERBAL EXPLOSIONS AND THE ADDITION OF NEW, VOCABULARY WORDS.**

- ❖ **SINCE EARLY ATTEMPTS TO SPEAK ARE FLEETING AND PRECIOUS, ENJOY EVERY BABBLING MOMENT.**

✳ Fostering Mathematical Skills

Some individuals seem to be mathematical wizards and others cannot grasp the skills at all. Controversy exists as to whether the ability to think mathematically using logic and spatial reasoning is inherited. Can the skills be stimulated from infancy? Since all knowledge is beneficial, it cannot hurt to try and introduce your infant, toddler, and young child to the basic mathematical components.

GIVE YOUR CHILD A HEAD START TOWARDS UNDERSTANDING MATHEMATICS: SHAPES, NUMBERS, AND MEASUREMENTS

✦ **HELP YOUR BABY LOOK AT SIMPLE SHAPES IN THE SURROUNDINGS TO INTRODUCE THE COMPONENTS OF GEOMETRY.** "Throw the round ball to Mommy." "This book is square." "Let's eat a pizza triangle.

TOYS WITH SIMPLE SHAPES INTRODUCE THE INFANT AND THE TODDLER TO GEOMETRIC FORMS AND EYE-HAND COORDINATION SKILLS.

✦ **REFER TO BODY PARTS AND ASK, "HOW MANY?" YOU ARE TEACHING YOUR CHILD HOW TO COUNT SOME-THING MEANINGFUL.** "Look at your face in the mirror. How many eyes do you have? 1- 2," "Ears? 1 - 2," "Hands? 1 - 2," "Feet? 1 - 2." "How many belly buttons? Only 1." "How many fingers do you have on one hand? 5"

✦ **COUNT FAMILIAR ITEMS AND BRING UNDERSTAND-ING TO NUMBERS.** Keep your child distracted until the food comes in a restaurant, by counting jelly or sugar packets, spoons, napkins, straws, or pictures on the menu. "How many books did we bring to read while we wait for our food? 1 - 2." "How many toys did we bring? 1-2-3. It is so much fun to count while we are waiting."

✦ **PREPARE FOOD IN THE KITCHEN AND TEACH ABOUT PARTS AND WHOLES.** For example, when preparing a cheese sandwich, teach about one whole square sandwich. Then cut the bread into halves on the diagonal and talk about the two triangles. Next day, make a square turkey sandwich and cut it in half horizon-tally into two rectangles. On the following day, cut a square tuna sandwich into quarters, four, small squares. When a circular pizza arrives, count those individual triangles that make the round shape. A child under five years of age will not grasp all those fractions imme-diately, but with weekly repetition, even a toddler may begin to recog-nize the shapes and the concept, "a whole is made up of all the parts."

✦ **FOLLOW A RECIPE AND DEMONSTRATE MEASUREMENT.** Ask your child to fill a cup with flour and pour it into a big bowl. Add 3 tablespoons of sugar, a half of a cup of water, etc. Break and add 6 eggs.

✦ **SLICE AND COUNT VEGETABLES OR FRUIT FOR A SALAD.** "How many tomato slices should we put in the salad?" "Count the cucumbers." "Dad has three peppers, one red, one yellow and one green." "Count the fresh broccoli or carrots." "Let's make a fruit salad with 6 strawberries, 8 melon balls, and 10 blueberries. Don't forget 1 pineapple ring."

✦ **ASK YOUR BABY TO STAND AGAINST A WALL TO MEA-SURE HEIGHT OR SEE THE NUMBERS ON A BATH-ROOM SCALE TO DETERMINE WEIGHT.** "How tall are you?" "How much do you weigh?" Then, Dad and Mom weigh and measure to compare little, big, and bigger.

✦ **POINT TO THE NUMBERS ON A CLOCK OR A WATCH. ALTHOUGH YOUNG CHILDREN CANNOT GRASP THE MATHEMATICAL CONCEPT OF TIME, THEY CAN BEGIN TO MAKE THE CONNECTION WHEN YOU SHOW THE CLOCK AT BATH TIME OR BEDTIME.**

✦ **TEACH SUBTRACTION AND ADDITION. LINE UP OBJECTS, TAKE AWAY ONE-AT-A-TIME, THEN BRING BACK ONE-AT-A-TIME.** You can play this "game" while waiting to eat. For example, line up four spoons. Take one away. "How many spoons do we have now?" Count, "One-two-three spoons are left." Take one more away. "What is left now?" Begin again and add a spoon to the line-up. Kids will love to play and not realize the mathematical knowledge they are capturing.

✦ **LOOK AT A CALENDAR WITH "LARGE" NUMBERS.** If your child can handle a crayon with some control (ages 3 1/2 - 4 years), encourage him to trace some of the numbers, or color the boxes around the numbers; name the numbers as your child highlights each one with color.

HELPFUL HINT:

FUN-FILLED FAMILY ACTIVITIES THAT INCLUDE LANGUAGE, MATHEMATICS, SCIENCE, SOCIAL STUDIES AND MORE WILL CREATE LASTING LEARNING ADVENTURES.

✻   **Discovering Science**

Children have an amazing, curious nature and love the "hands-on, nose and tongues-in" approach to learning about life. They are interested in everyone and everything including plants, animals, insects, the sky, stars, sun, moon and the ocean.

ENCOURAGE AWARENESS OF THE SELF AND UNDERSTANDING OF THE WORLD AS YOU EXPLORE LIFE WITH YOUR CHILD

☐ **HELP YOUR YOUNGSTER DISCOVER THE FIVE SENSES:**
Sharpen your child's sensations as you encourage him/her to look, listen, touch, taste, and smell. Try these simple games of identification:

- Look around the kitchen. "I see a yellow banana. Can your eyes see it, too?"

- Close your eyes in an Italian restaurant. "Can your nose smell the garlic rolls?"

- Listen together in a quiet room. "Can your ears hear the ticking clock?"

- In the Southwestern restaurant, ask, "Can your tongue taste the salty chips?"

- While holding a stuffed animal, ask "Can your fingers feel your soft doggy?"

☐ **TEACH THE CONCEPT OF DISSOLVING:** Make instant pudding together by adding two cups of milk to a chocolate "powder" mix. Your child can stir and watch the mixture change its form. Allow your child to watch as you carefully add boiling water to flavored gelatin. Your toddler will observe the same "powder disappearing" effect.

☐ **DEMONSTRATE HOW SUBSTANCES CHANGE WITH TEMPERATURE CHANGES:**

- Place the pudding or Jell-O mixture into the cold refrigerator and watch the dessert become thick and cold.

- Pour orange juice into four cups, add wooden pop sticks, place them into the freezer and discover four, frozen treats an hour later.

- Place cold slices of cheese on two pieces of bread, put them into the toaster, and watch the heat melt the cheese on the bread.

☐ **IF YOU HAVE A PET, TEACH YOUR CHILD TO HELP WITH THE CARE, THUS STIMULATING AN INTEREST IN ANIMAL LIFE:** "Birds need water and food, just like you." "Our doggy needs a bath, just like you." "All pets need love, just like you."

☐ **PLANT SEEDS TOGETHER IN A POT ON THE WINDOW SILL OR IN THE GARDEN AND DEVELOP A LOVE FOR THINGS THAT GROW.** Orange or grapefruit pits or lima beans grow quickly. Cut a piece from the bottom of a carrot (where the greens come up), place it in water, and watch new leaves sprout up

☐ **EXPLORE NATURE AND THE WORLD:** Discuss the sun, moon, stars, rain, clouds, thunder, and lightning. Visit animals in the pet store, on the farm, and in the zoo. You and your youngster will love the variety.

2. Teaching Creativity: Music, Melodies, Movement, and Art

✳ Listening and Participating

Some individuals enjoy music, the theater, and art as observers, while others become creative participants. In an effort to develop your son or daughter's prospective abilities, introduce the arts in the early years; your child will define his/her own involvement in the future.

PRESENT YOUR YOUNG CHILD WITH CREATIVE OPPORTUNI-TIES AND ENCOURAGE A WELL-ROUNDED PERSONALITY

☐ **BRING MUSIC INTO YOUR HOME TO DEVELOP A LOVE FOR HARMONY AND SONG AND RECEIVE THE BENEFITS OF AN INHERENT CALMING EFFECT.** Listen to a music box, a musical mobile, CDs, the radio, a concert on TV, and someone playing an instrument. Mix classical, popular, and instrumental tunes.

The notion that classical music, particularly the high frequency sounds of a Mozart melody will stimulate the brain and improve mathematical abilities has been explored as "The Mozart Effect for Children."

Furthermore, a research team at the University of California (Irvine) found that pre-school children with eight months of musical training on a keyboard enhanced their spatial reasoning ability.

Still, other studies link music to intellectual and creative development, improved concentration, and coordination. Some musical videos for infants have been based on these theories.

☐ **TEACH YOUR INFANT OR TODDLER TO EXPERIMENT WITH SOUND. EXPERIENCES WITH A PIANO, GUITAR, DRUM, XYLOPHONE, OR A SIMPLE POT AND SPOON WILL ENCOURAGE MUSICAL TALENT.** Your child willlove to keep the beat. Ask your little one to, "Shake, shake" a box of rice or pasta and watch the smiles.

"LOOK AT ME! I'M HAVING FUN." MATH ABILITIES ARE DEVELOPING, TOO.

☐ **DANCE WITH YOUR CHILD, SWIRL AROUND, FEEL RHYTHM, MOVEMENT, AND ROCK TO THE MUSIC.** Persuade your son or daughter to sway, bounce, jump, or hop like a bunny to a musical CD.

☐ **ATTEND AN AGE-APPROPRIATE CONCERT, CHILDREN'S SHOW, SHORT DANCE PERFORMANCE, OR SKATING PROGRAM.** Since most children under three years cannot sit for long, take an aisle seat. Leave when your youngster seems impatient. Stay just long enough to make it fun and hope to extend the experience the following time.

❋   **Looking and Exploring**

⌘ **TEACH YOUR CHILD TO BE OBSERVANT AND DEVELOP AN APPRECIATION FOR ART BY BRINGING PAINTINGS AND SCULPTURE INTO YOUR HOME DÉCOR; LOOK AT THE ARTWORK TOGETHER.** "See the red flowers. Look at the little girl in the picture. She's wearing a blue dress." "Can you find the green trees in the picture?" "Do you see the white dog in the painting?"

⌘ **TAKE YOUR YOUNGSTER TO A MUSEUM FOR MUSICAL OR ARTISTIC DISCOVERY**. Most cities offer specialty, children's museums or designate areas in large museums for fun, hands-on, youth activities. When planning a vacation, check the Chamber of Commerce guidebook for an appropriate adventure in the area.

⌘ **HELP YOUR SON OR DAUGHTER PAY ATTENTION TO THE BEAUTY OF NATURE, THE SHAPES AND COLORS IN THE ENVIRONMENT.** "Look at the blue sky. The green trees are reaching to the fluffy clouds." Your child will learn to appreciate the harmony of hue and the natural, artistic forms all around us.

⌘ **HELP YOUR CHILD DISCOVER "HANDS-ON" ACTIVITIES:**

- **YOUR INFANT CAN TOUCH, SQUISH, AND SWIRL DRY OATMEAL, RICE, OR COOKED PASTA IN A BOX OR PLASTIC CONTAINER.**

- **INTRODUCE YOUR TODDLER (18 -24 MONTHS) TO CRAYONS.** Move each color around the paper and make a circle: the sun, or a "happy face." Hold your little one's hand with a crayon and encourage him/her to move the colors, too. Trace her fingers on the paper. Trace his foot on a paper on the floor.

- **OFFER YOUR TODDLER SOME NON-TOXIC CLAY OR "PLAY DOH" FOR SQUEEZING, PULLING, ROLLING, AND TEARING. YOUR CHILD WILL STRENGTHEN HIS/HER "FINGER" MUSCLES NECESSARY FOR WRITING, CUTTING, BUTTONING BUTTONS, SNAPPING, ZIPPING, ETC.**

- **HAVE YOUR PRE-SCHOOL CHILD "FINGERPAINT" ON A PAPER OR A LARGE PAPER PLATE WITH CHOCOLATE PUDDING. IT WILL BE FUN (AND SAFE) TO LICK EVERY FINGER WHEN THE PICTURE IS DONE.**

HOMEMADE "PLAY" DOUGH

Blend: 1½ cups of flour
½ cup of salt
¼ cup of water
¼ cup of oil

Mix and knead to make a smooth, workable ball. (To reuse, save in a plastic bag or sealed container.)

Your son or daughter will love to feel the assorted textures and will gain a sense of control when he/she produces "a work of art." You will, of course, need to supervise and come prepared with water and paper towels or wipes for clean up.

3. Teaching Social Studies

To help your child gain knowledge of the world, first assist him in understanding himself. Every little boy or girl is preoccupied with, "ME," first. As you experience life with your growing young-ster, you can progressively expand learning from the self outwards.

TEACH YOUR CHILD ABOUT HIMSELF, THE FAMILY, THE NEIGHBORHOOD, OUR COUNTRY, AND FOREIGN LANDS

❋ **ME: SELF-DISCOVERY CAN BEGIN WHEN YOUR CHILD IS AN INFANT.**

- **LOOK IN THE MIRROR TOGETHER AND NAME, "EYES, EARS, NOSE, TONGUE, MOUTH, HAIR, HANDS, FEET, BELLY BUTTON, AND OTHER BODY PARTS."** Teach your child to look at his reflection as he brushes his hair and teeth.

- **WHILE IN THE BATHTUB, ENCOURAGE YOUR TODDLER TO WASH WITH A SOFT CLOTH OR SPONGE, AS YOU IDENTIFY EACH AREA.** For example, you can sing to the tune of, "London Bridges Falling Down." "Now it's time to wash your neck, wash your neck, wash your neck, Now it's time to wash your neck, And make it nice and clean." Sing about knees, elbows, toes, etc. Make good grooming (cleaning ears, cutting nails) fun.

- **HELP YOUR CHILD LEARN HOW BODY PARTS WORK:**
    - *Listen with your ears:* Ring a bell gently or put a ticking clock near your little one's ear.

    - *Smell with your nose:* Place an orange slice or a slice of pizza near your child's nose.

    - *Taste with your tongue:* Provide a salty pretzel, a sour lemon slice, or a sweet cookie to compare.

    - *Shake your head,* "No. No." **Nod,** " Yes. Yes."

    - **Clap - clap - clap your hands:** Open and shut them. Wiggle your fingers.

> ◆   *Bend your elbows and bend your knees.*

> ◆   *Stomp your feet.*

- **REFLECT YOUR CHILD'S FEELINGS TO HELP HIM LEARN ABOUT HIMSELF:** "I know you are hungry, but we must wait one more minute for your chicken to cool down. It's too hot." Or, "I know you feel tired. Let's get your pajamas."

❂ **THE FAMILY: EVEN DURING YOUR CHILD'S FIRST YEAR, HE/SHE CAN LEARN TO DISTINGUISH THE IMPORTANT, STABLE PEOPLE IN YOUR LIVES.**

- **PLACE PHOTOS OF YOUR YOUNGSTER AND ALL THE CLOSE RELATIVES IN FULL VIEW AROUND YOUR HOME, IN FRAMES, WITH MAGNETS ON THE REFRIGERATOR AT YOUR CHILD'S EYE LEVEL, AND ON THE WALLS OF HIS/HER ROOM. INCLUDE NANNIES AND BABY SITTERS.**

- **CREATE AND SHARE A PHOTO ALBUM WITH YOUR SON OR DAUGHTER.** Relax on the sofa, side by side, and as you look at each picture, try to form an association for your child. "Remember, Aunt Bridget took you to the park? Look at the picture. Who's pushing you on the swing?" "Here's Grandpa in front of his house. He lives far away and loves to see you. What does he call you when he visits? Sweetie! That's right."

- **PLAN FREQUENT FAMILY VISITS, SPECIAL OCCASION CELEBRATIONS, OR SIMPLY ARRANGE TO MEET AT A COMMON LOCATION FOR AN ACTIVITY EVERYONE WILL ENJOY.**

- **WATCH HOMEMADE VIDEOS TOGETHER OF FAMILY FUN EVENTS.**

- **USING TODAY'S ADVANCED TECHNOLOGY, COMMUNICATE VIA VIDEO CONFERENCING (video cameras connect to each computer.)**

- **WHEN CHILDREN LEARN TO TYPE, THEY CAN E-MAIL RELATIVES.**

- **PHONE FAMILY MEMBERS SEVERAL TIMES A WEEK TO HELP YOUR CHILD FEEL CLOSE TO THEM AND PROVIDE AN EXTRA FEELING OF SECURITY AND DEPENDABILITY.**

❁ **THE NEIGHBORHOOD: INCLUDE YOUR CHILD IN WALKS AROUND YOUR HOME, TO LOCAL SHOPPING FACILITIES AND EATERIES. TALK ABOUT THE PEOPLE YOU MEET.** "This is the lady who delivers the mail. Let's say, "Thank you for this letter from Aunt Paula." "This man sells groceries. We need to buy milk and bread today." "Let's visit the shoe store and the lady will help us find the right shoe that fits you." Refer to the policeman, fireman, doctor, dentist, etc. Point out related vehicles and sirens, and discuss different jobs when each opportunity arises.

❁ **OUR LAND: THE CONCEPT OF OUR NATION IS TOO ABSTRACT FOR A YOUNG CHILD, BUT HE/SHE CAN LEARN TO RECOGNIZE OUR FLAG, THE COLORS, STRIPES, AND STARS.**

- **IF FAMILY MEMBERS ARE IN DIFFERENT STATES, YOU CAN NAME THOSE PLACES.** "Grandma and Pa live in Florida. We live in New York." **A CHILD OF THREE YEARS OLD, OR OLDER, MIGHT ENJOY LOOKING AT A GLOBE.** "If we take an airplane and visit Uncle Charles, we start here and go up to there." Discuss the weather. "Cousin Jane lives here where it is always warm. We live here and sometimes it gets very cold."

- **AS YOU INCLUDE YOUR CHILD IN YOUR TRAVELS OR VACATION PLANS, YOU PROVIDE OPPORTUNITIES TO LEARN ABOUT TRANSPORTATION VEHICLES, DIFFERENT PARTS OF OUR COUNTRY, THE CLIMATE, PLACES OF INTEREST, AND THE PEOPLE.**

❀ **AROUND THE WORLD: INTRODUCE YOUR SON OR DAUGHTER TO THE IDEA THAT THERE ARE PEOPLE FAR AWAY, ACROSS THE OCEAN.** "On the other side of the world, there is a little girl or boy who is being hugged and kissed by a mom and dad. Everyone needs to eat, sleep, and have a family and friends to love."

- **READ STORIES ABOUT CHILDREN IN OTHER LANDS.**

- **TASTE INTERNATIONAL FOODS:** Italian pizza, pasta, French toast, fries, Chinese vegetables, noodles, Mexican chips and salsa, Israeli falafel.

- **LISTEN TO INSTRUMENTAL MUSIC AND VOCALISTS SINGING IN FOREIGN LANGUAGES.**

- **VIEW DANCING AND COSTUMES ON INTERNATIONAL VIDEOS, AT FAIRS, OR IN DISNEY WORLD, ORLANDO, FLORIDA ("IT'S A SMALL WORLD").**

"He's Got The Whole World in His Hands"

4. Setting a Good Example for Etiquette, Values and Social Skills

As an influential teacher, you will not only help your son or daughter gain an understanding of himself, his family, neighborhood, country, and the world, you will also build self-confidence, independence, and develop the other skills necessary to socialize with the people he meets

✳ Politeness and Manners

YOU ARE RESPONSIBLE FOR PREPARING YOUR CHILD TO FUNCTION APPROPRIATELY IN OUR SOCIETY AND THIS "SOCIALIZATION PROCESS" BEGINS IN INFANCY. YOUR OUTLOOK ON LIFE, YOUR VALUES AND ATTITUDES TOWARDS OTHERS, AND WHETHER YOU OBEY THE RULES OF SOCIETY WILL IMPACT YOUR IMPRESSIONABLE YOUNGSTER. If you behave insensitively and express an, 'I don't care about you' manner, do not be surprised when your child becomes selfish and rude. If your spouse behaves stubbornly, and is occasionally discourteous, don't be shocked when your youngster throws tantrums or is disrespectful to others.

HELPFUL HINT:

TO INSTILL WELL-MANNERED AND COURTEOUS BEHAVIOR IN YOUR CHILD, BE POLITE AND CONSIDERATE OF OTHERS. SAY, "PLEASE, THANK YOU, EXCUSE ME, LET'S SHARE," AND YOUR YOUNGSTER WILL REPEAT YOUR EXAMPLE.

When your toddler starts pre-school, the teachers will be impressed with the child who is respectful and cooperative and the other kids will seek his/her friendship.

✳ Honesty and Morality

It is more difficult to teach your child to be honest, moral, and ethical than it is to teach him/her to express a few socially proper words, like "Please and Thank you." The values you set will determine the way your youngster interacts with others.

Lorna pushed her young daughter in the shopping cart and as they passed the produce, she always took a piece of fruit for each of them to eat. She never paid for those items, yet surprisingly didn't think she was stealing.

Years later, her daughter, nine years old, put a bracelet on her wrist as they passed the jewelry counter in a department store and kept walking until the store security guard stopped them and called the police. Lorna was held responsible for her young child's actions. "I cannot believe that my child would take something without paying for it," Lorna cried.

If you are deceitful, do not be surprised if your child is underhanded. If you lie to your son or daughter, don't be shocked when he/she is untruthful to you. If you ignore traffic signals, slip in front of people waiting in line, use loud, malicious language in public places, expect your child to be equally discourteous, aggressive, shrill, and sneaky.

HELPFUL HINT:

TO MAINTAIN ORDER, EVERY SOCIETY ESTABLISHES LAWS AND YOU, THE PARENT, ARE RESPONSIBLE FOR TEACHING YOUR CHILD TO COMPLY WITH THESE SOCIAL STANDARDS; YOUR WORDS AND ACTIONS WILL GUIDE YOUR YOUNGSTER'S BEHAVIOR.

✳ Unwritten Laws of Humanity

IN EACH CULTURE, THERE ARE UNWRITTEN LAWS OF CIVILIZATION THAT ARE CUSTOMARILY UNDERSTOOD, SUCH AS BEING HELPFUL TO THE DISABLED OR CHARITABLE TO THE LESS FORTUNATE. YOUR BEHAVIOR AND COMMENTS IN THIS REGARD, WILL EITHER ESTABLISH A SENSE OF CARING AND GENEROSITY IN YOUR CHILD'S CHARACTER, OR A LACK OF BENEVOLENCE TOWARDS OTHERS. If you open your home to friends and family and extend hospitality and experiences of sharing, you will encourage your child to be kind to others. If you choose to remain isolated and detached, your child will act aloof, unfriendly, and probably be suspicious of others.

❋ Good Grooming and Personal Hygiene

IN SOCIAL SETTINGS, PEOPLE ENJOY THOSE FOLKS WHO LOOK PRESENTABLE AND SMELL CLEAN. PERSONAL HYGIENE AND CLEANLINESS SHOULD BECOME AN INTEGRAL PART OF YOUR CHILD'S DAILY ROUTINES FROM INFANCY ONWARD. When you set a good example with sanitary health habits, your child will model your lead.

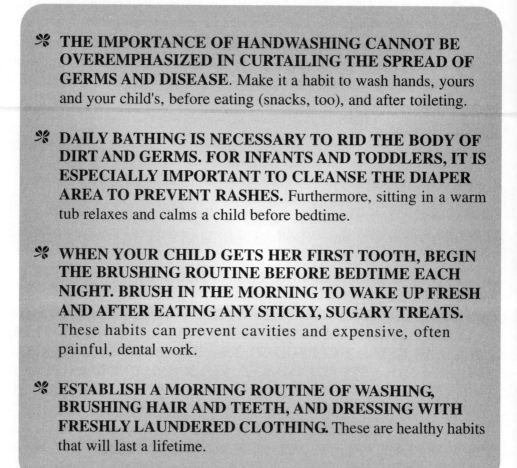

❋ THE IMPORTANCE OF HANDWASHING CANNOT BE OVEREMPHASIZED IN CURTAILING THE SPREAD OF GERMS AND DISEASE. Make it a habit to wash hands, yours and your child's, before eating (snacks, too), and after toileting.

❋ DAILY BATHING IS NECESSARY TO RID THE BODY OF DIRT AND GERMS. FOR INFANTS AND TODDLERS, IT IS ESPECIALLY IMPORTANT TO CLEANSE THE DIAPER AREA TO PREVENT RASHES. Furthermore, sitting in a warm tub relaxes and calms a child before bedtime.

❋ WHEN YOUR CHILD GETS HER FIRST TOOTH, BEGIN THE BRUSHING ROUTINE BEFORE BEDTIME EACH NIGHT. BRUSH IN THE MORNING TO WAKE UP FRESH AND AFTER EATING ANY STICKY, SUGARY TREATS. These habits can prevent cavities and expensive, often painful, dental work.

❋ ESTABLISH A MORNING ROUTINE OF WASHING, BRUSHING HAIR AND TEETH, AND DRESSING WITH FRESHLY LAUNDERED CLOTHING. These are healthy habits that will last a lifetime.

5. Teaching Responsibility, Ambition, Goals, Expectations

✳ Teaching Responsibility

Most children love to cooperate and please an adult. Even a child of two or three can learn to be conscientious and dependable. Begin at your house.

TEACH YOUR LITTLE ONE TO HELP WITH SIMPLE TASKS AT HOME

Ask your child to get involved, to participate in small jobs around your home and he/she will feel important, capable, and part of the family. As your youngster matures, this feeling of commitment, cooperation, and loyalty will increase and extend to others outside the family.

WATERING THE PLANTS IS FUN FOR THE TODDLER AS SHE LEARNS RESPONSIBILITY.

☙ **HOUSEHOLD CHORES:** Your toddler can help you wipe a spill, put toys in a box, or set the table. "Please put the napkin and the spoon on the placemat and I'll put down the fork and knife." In the garden, "Let's water the flowers and help them grow."

☙ **CARE FOR PETS:** "Get the doggie's soap and we'll give her a bath." "Help Daddy feed the fish." "You can put some water in Kitty's bowl." A boy or girl who is not expected to clean up after playing or help with the household chores and family responsibilities will not rise to the occasion when asked to help in a friend's home or at school. This child will be irresponsible and undependable.

HELPFUL HINT:

IF YOU ARE A RESPONSIBLE PUBLIC CITIZEN, CONSIDERATE OF THE LAW AND HUMAN RIGHTS, YOUR CHILD WILL FOLLOW YOUR LEAD:

❖ Ask your daughter to listen courteously as you read or tell a story and she will learn to respect authority figures (family, teachers, performers, etc.).

❖ Ask your son to help you as you hold the door open for an elderly man or a disabled lady and he will become compassionate and socially responsible.

❋ **Teaching Ambition and Setting Realistic Goals**

To fulfill, "The American Dream," an individual must have the opportunity and the ambition. How can you inspire your child with motivation and the desire to succeed?

IF ARE CONSCIENTIOUS, YOUR SON OR DAUGHTER WILL BECOME AMBITIOUS TOO. IF YOU PREFER TO DELAY CHORES, IGNORE RESPONSIBILITY AND CHOOSE NOT TO WORK, YOUR CHILD WILL MODEL THAT CAREFREE, NON-COMMITAL MIND-SET.

YOUR ATTITUDE AND YOUR STANDARDS WILL INFLUENCE YOUR CHILD'S CHARACTER:

- **TEACH AMBITION AND PRIDE:** If you are energetic and believe that hard work leads to achievement, your child will under stand the importance of effort and motivation. When you express pleasure in fulfilling your own endeavors, your child will learn about pride in accomplishment. Most successful children have watched a determined parent work at home or on the job.

- **TEACH ABOUT HOPES, DREAMS, AND FAMILY VALUES:** When your child is old enough to understand, share your desires, wishes, and the realities of achieving dreams. "We wish we could have a bigger house so everyone will have some personal space, but we are lucky to have our wonderful family. We love each other and that is more important than having that big house."

- **TEACH THE VALUE OF MONEY:** Explain, "We need money for food, clothing, toys, and other things we want, but we must work very hard to earn those dollars. That's why Daddy and Mommy go to work everyday."

Each Sunday morning, Harry and his two-year-old son picked up bagels, orange juice, and other breakfast foods for the family. Dad handed little Jack a $20 bill to give to the store clerk. The boy soon learned the concept of "paying for purchases."

When you teach the value of money, you may find it difficult to explain that life involves choices and compromise. "You cannot have every thing you want."

When Megan turned five, she received cash from her grandparents. "I want to buy a doll house, a doll, and a paint set with my birthday money."

"I'm sorry," explained her mother in the toy store. "We do not have enough to buy it all, but you have a choice. You can have one big doll house, or two smaller things." The child came to understand that the same amount of money can be used in different ways.

- **SET REALISTIC GOALS:** Even a small child can work towards completing a small household task or a little assignment outside the home. Applaud all efforts and your youngster will feel proud.

For example, Sandy asked her four year old to place mats on the table. "Put one near each chair and put a napkin on each mat." When the little girl was done, Sandy hugged her, kissed her and praised, "You did a great job." The goal was reasonable, reachable, and repeatable each evening. The child also learned that she was an important member of the family with a responsible job.

✱ Raising Expectations

Two weeks later, Sandy asked her daughter to also bring the bread and butter to the table. "What else can I do?" asked the girl when she completed the job. She felt quite important and motivated to do more; it was time to raise the expectations and set additional objectives.

✱ Creating Enthusiasm for Achievement

YOUR ATTITUDE CAN INFLUENCE YOUR CHILD'S GOALS, HIS/HER EAGERNESS OR INDIFFERENCE FOR ACCOMPLISHMENT.

Liam tried out for the swim team and was full of excitement. "I made it and only six kids were chosen!" he screamed when his Dad picked him up after tryouts. "I need to get to school by 7:30 a.m. each morning for practice."

His Dad beamed, "I'm proud of you, son, and wish I could take you each day, but unfortunately, I need to leave for work by 6:15 a.m. I'm sure Mom will drive you."

While Liam's Dad was quite ambitious, his mother was apathetic and lazy. "Forget it! I'm not getting up that early for you to go swimming. Wait until you're older and drive yourself."

This mother ignored the first secret of perfect parenting, "Prioritize! Your child's well-being is your first priority." Liam's swimming activities would help him grow physically and participation in the sport would help him feel good about himself. Instead, his talent was not developed and his passion died. Liam felt that his mother didn't care about him or his aptitude. In actuality, she lacked respect for her child and thought more about her own inconvenience than his achievement.

❋ Respecting Your Child's Goals

Occasionally, a parent will have an ambitious plan for his child that does not coincide with the capabilities of the son or daughter.

Mitch was on the track team when he was in high school and expected his son, Buddy, to be excited about running too. "Dad, I can't run as fast as the other guys. I have short legs, but I'm coordinated and would probably be great at playing tennis." Buddy earnestly proposed a more realistic athletic goal for himself and although his Dad was disappointed at first, he soon began watching tennis on TV with his son. Before long, Bud was competing and Mitch was cheering for the activity of his sons' choosing.

HELPFUL HINT:

IF YOUR CHILD IS NOT INTERESTED IN MEETING YOUR GOALS, BUT IS EAGER TO ACHIEVE IN ANOTHER, INDEPENDENT WAY, ACT MATURELY, RESPECT AND ENCOURAGE YOUR CHILD'S AMBITION.

6. Teaching Decision-Making, Independence

Ella always wanted to be the boss and didn't permit her husband, Stanley, to make decisions. Weak and indecisive, because he grew up with a controlling mother, Stanley accepted his domineering wife and became a poor role model for their two sons. Unfortunately, Ella treated her boys the same way she treated Stanley. She would tell them what to wear, eat, and whom to see.

The boys, now in their teens, felt that their opinions were of little value. By making all the decisions, Ella stripped her "guys" of self-confidence, independence and self-motivation. They would forever be without the skills of thinking, planning, and decision-making, all necessary for success in life.

Although you may feel that you know what is best for your child, it is important to prepare your son or daughter to reason, make choices, and solve problems independently. This process begins in the early years and is important for emotional maturation.

❋ Supporting Your Child's Choices

Many toddlers and pre-schoolers have likes, and dislikes. It is up to you to provide your youngster with various opportunities to make selections; then respect those choices and show your child that you value his/her thoughts.

Brenda had a talk with her four-year-old daughter, Lindsay. "We're going to have a barbeque on Sunday with Daddy's friends, but you may invite one of your friends to join us: Kevin and his Mom and Dad or Jaclyn and her folks. Which family would you like me to call?"

The day before the party, Dad asked Lindsay, "Would you like to help us plan the menu? We can have burgers or chicken, fries or corn on the cob? Do you know what Jaclyn likes to eat?"

When Lindsay's parents allowed her to take an active role in planning the family's event, she felt very important. Her parents followed through by accepting her decisions.

YOU CAN ENCOURAGE THE DEVELOPMENT OF LEADERSHIP TRAITS, INDEPENDENT THINKING, THE ABILITY TO MAKE CHOICES, AND FEELINGS OF SELF-CONFIDENCE:

❖ Give your child opportunities to choose between acceptable options.

❖ Recognize your child's preferences if they are reasonable *(You still retain supervision by providing the choices).*

✳ **Accepting Independent Thought**

When toddlers develop opinions, they often enter into power struggles with their parents. Frequently, clashes revolve around insignificant issues, but the unpleasant tone of the conflict lasts for years to come. Avoid arguing over trivial concerns.

Marnie wanted her daughter, Alana, to wear her patent leather party shoes to her friend's birthday event, but Alana refused. "I want my sandals!" shouted the three-year-old and commotion ensued.

When Grandma arrived she clued her daughter, "You were the same as Alana, a kid who knew what she wanted. That's why you succeeded in life." Marnie smiled and said, "Honestly, it really doesn't matter whether she wears her party shoes or her sandals to that birthday party. Why am I fighting with her? She may have a real reason for her preference."

She called to her daughter to reveal her change of mind. "Alana, you can wear your sandals if you like them better than your patent shoes." Alana was overjoyed. "I will also have more fun at the party. Those shiny shoes hurt my feet."

DO NOT ENGAGE IN DAILY POWER STRUGGLES OVER, "MY WAY vs. YOUR WAY." DEVELOP A LOVING, COMMUNICATIVE, AND TOLERANT RELATIONSHIP AND PRAISE YOUR CHILD FOR HAVING IDEAS, SELF-ASSURANCE, PERSONAL PREFERENCES, AND AN ENTHUSIASTIC SPIRIT.

Highlights

"T" = "TEACH, TEACH, TEACH" SELF-AWARENESS AND KNOWLEDGE OF THE WORLD; YOU AND YOUR SPOUSE ARE YOUR CHILD'S FIRST AND MOST IMPORTANT TEACHERS.

1. Teach intellectual skills through everyday experiences.

2. Teach creativity by exposing your child to art, movement, and music..

3. Teach social skills, manners, good grooming, morality, and honesty, through practice and by your example.

4. Teach ambition and goal setting by acting as a role model and encouraging your child's accomplishments.

5. Teach emotional strength, family values, decision-making, independence, and the value of money, by respecting your youngster's thoughts and choices.

The Seven Secrets of P-E-R-F-E-C-T Parenting Are Revealed

c o n c l u s i o n

Although parenting is a difficult and often puzzling job, it is incredibly rewarding and fulfilling to share in the development of your child from a helpless, dependent infant, to an increasingly independent toddler, to a thriving young child, to a growing teen, and ultimately, to a successful, self-sufficient, and lovable young adult.

HELPFUL HINT:

LIFE'S STAGES PASS QUICKLY. TAKE THE TIME TO ADORE AND ENJOY YOUR YOUNGSTER DURING EVERY PHASE OF YOUR LIVES.

Revealed through each letter of the word, **"P-E-R-F-E-C-T,"** the seven secrets will help you raise productive and caring children. Although total perfection is impossible, *you can't be the perfect parent, nor can your son or daughter be the perfect child,* the desire to be really outstanding is an admiral goal and will lead you in the right direction:

1. **"P"= PRIORITIZE:** Design "Priority pie," a weekly plan to help you and your spouse understand one another and balance your family's needs, responsibilities, and desires in order of significance; **YOUR CHILD'S WELL-BEING IS FIRST.** Provide your son or daughter with basic care, love, comfort, security, and a happy, organized home environment. As you plan your seven-day agenda, consider marriage, parenting, pet care, career, family obligations, social events, relaxation, and personal fulfillment.

2. **"E" = EXPERIENCE LIFE WITH YOUR CHILD:** Introduce your youngster to our world and share in the excitement of exploring the environment through the senses. Enjoy the sights, sounds, smells, tastes, and touch of new things and places. Partake in a variety of age-appropriate events. Respect your little one as an intelligent human being and exchange thoughts, ideas, and opinions.

   When you cannot be there for your son or daughter, select a competent Caregiver to take your place in a quality environment. Also, plan ahead and set the stage for valuable experiences.

3. **"R"="ROUTINIZE,"** but do not **"ROBOTIZE:"** Set routines, rules, limits, and guidelines to help organize your busy lives and establish discipline, personal responsibility, and social expectations. Healthy individuals are adaptable, creative, and flexible within their orderly world; therefore, encourage occasional changes and choices.

4. **"F"= FOLLOW THROUGH:** To insure consistency, a sense of security, and honesty, make promises that you can keep, rules that the entire family will honor, expectations that are realistic. When you routinely follow through, you teach your youngster that you are dependable.

5. **"E" = ENCOURAGE:** Develop your child's strengths, overcome weaknesses and he/she will thrive intellectually, physically, emotionally, socially, and creatively. Praise current accomplishments to encourage future achievements. Be a role model for your son or daughter. As you give your time and dedication, you will also demonstrate the values of commitment and responsibility.

6. **"C"= COMMUNICATE:** When you pay attention to feelings, facial expressions, body language, to "what is said" and "what is not said," you open the lines of communication between you and your child and feel "in-sync," connected. As your child grows, encourage the expression of individual feelings, ideas, and establish sincere and honest exchanges. Create a loving, democratic climate and always remain available to listen and help with decision-making. You will feel close to your child whether you are near or far.

7. **"T" = TEACH, TEACH, TEACH:** You are your child's first and most important teacher conveying knowledge, emotional strength, social experiences, morals, ethics, and values. You teach by communicating, by living life together, and by providing a positive role model.

DELIGHT IN EVERY MAGICAL MOMENT WITH YOUR

CHILD AND YOUR PARENTING JOB WILL BE

P-E-R-F-E-C-TLY SUCCESSFUL.

References

Ainsworth, M.D.S, Bell, S.M., and Stayton, D.J. (1971) 'Individual differences in strange situation behavior of one-year-olds,' in H.R. Schaffer (ed.) The Origins of Human Social Relations, 17-57, London: Academic Press.

American Academy of Pediatrics. Task Force on Infant Sleep Position and Sudden Infant Death Syndrome. Pediatrics. Vol. 105, #3, March 2000, pp. 650 - 656.

Bowlby, John. (1988) A Secure Base. Parent-Child Attachment and Healthy Human Development. New York: Basic Books.

Campbell, Don. The Mozart Effect. Avon Books (1977)

Erikson, Erik, H. Childhood and Society. W.W. Norton and Company. New York: 1950.

Gardner, Howard. Intelligence Reframed: Multiple Intelligences for the 21st Century. New York: Basic, 2000.

Gray, John, Ph.D. Children Are From Heaven. New York: HarperCollins, 1999.

Harlow, Harry F. "The Nature of Love." Reviewed in Haimowitz & Haimowitz, Human Development Selected Readings (New York: Thomas Y. Crowell Company, 1960), pp. 190-206.

http://www.babycenter.com.

http://www.nagc.org/ParentInfo/index.html National Association for Gifted Children. "Parent Information, Who are the Gifted?"

http://www.ri.net/gifted_talented/character.html "Characteristics and Behaviors of the Gifted."

http://www.safechild.net/for_parent/diet and nutrition.html

http://www.kinderstart.com. Food & Nutrition; "USDA Food Guide Pyramid for Young Children."

http://www.nms.on.ca/Elementary/know_your_nutrients. Nutritional Management Services; "Know Your Nutrients."

http://.geocites.com/Heartland/Pointe/5929/prelangdev.html. "Stages of Language Development."

Levine, Mel, M.D. A Mind at a Time. New York: Simon & Schuster, 2002.

Liebert, Robert M. and Spiegler, Michael D. Personality. Strategies and Issues. California: Brooks/Cole Publishing (1990) pp. 94-5.

Mason, Linda. The Working Mother's Guide to Life. New York: Three Rivers Press, 2002.

Moorehead, Joanna. KISS Guide to Baby & Child Care. London: Dorling Kindersley, 2002.

Rauscher, Shaw, Levine, Ky, & Wright, "Music & Spatial Task Performance." University of California, Irvine, 1994.

i n d e x . . .